For the Whole of Creation

For the Whole of Creation

*Christianity and Scholarship
in the Public Square, the Guild,
and the Church*

Edited by John Steven Paul
and James Paul Old

Published by Valparaiso University Press, Valparaiso, IN 46383

First Edition: First printing September 2010

Cover design: Becca Spivak Hendricks

TABLE OF CONTENTS

KEYNOTE ADDRESS

Foreword

S ince its inception in the early 1990s, the Lilly Fellows Program in Humanities and the Arts (LFP) has sought to renew and enhance the connections between Christianity and the academic vocation at church-related colleges and universities. It has done so through two primary means: stimulating a national conversation about questions and issues facing Christian higher education and preparing young teacher-scholars for careers at church-related colleges and universities.

To cultivate this conversation about Christian higher education, the LFP has provided numerous opportunities to bring faculty and administrators from a wide range of church-related institutions together, face-to-face. The primary vehicle for such encounters is the LFP National Network of church-related schools, which has grown from twenty-five members at its beginning in October 1991 to ninety-three in 2010. Since that first October meeting, representatives of these network schools have gathered annually at a national conference to explore issues of church-related higher education. Supported generously by the Lilly Endowment Inc. and by dues from member schools, the LFP, under the guidance of its staff and a national board, has provided grants among these network schools to support regional conferences, research conferences, summer seminars focused on teaching, on-campus mentoring of new faculty in church-related mission, and opportunities to exchange best practices. Each year, the LFP also brings together senior administrators from network schools for a workshop on church-related mission. The ninety-three member schools in the network represent a diversity of denominational traditions, institutional types, and geographic locations.

To further the goal of preparing young scholars for careers at church-related institutions, in the fall of 1992, the LFP sponsored the first cohort of Lilly Postdoctoral Fellows, who embarked on two-year residential fellowships at Valparaiso University. There have since been nineteen cohorts of Lilly Fellows—fifty-six Lilly Fellows in all—who have taken time at the outset of their careers to hone their teaching skills, receive mentoring from established teacher-scholars, pursue their research agendas, and reflect on how their own careers might connect to the larger mission of Christian higher education. With the initial support of Lilly Endowment Inc., as well as the continued support of Valparaiso University, the Lilly Fellows Program attracts nearly two hundred applicants each year.

Given the success of the Lilly Postdoctoral Fellows Program, it made sense to extend this program to graduate students. So in 2008, the LFP launched the Lilly Graduate Fellows Program, which supports young men and women who have bachelor's degrees from LFP Network Schools and are interested in becoming teacher-scholars at church-related colleges and universities. Each year, the Lilly Graduate Fellows Program selects a cohort of sixteen Fellows, of which there have now been three, who will be entering graduate school the following fall. Over a three-year period, these Fellows, along with two senior mentors, communicate and collaborate with each other in areas of research, teaching, and professional development.

As the LFP has matured over its nearly twenty-year history, the two primary components—conversation and leadership development—have overlapped. As its founders had hoped, not only have many Lilly Postdoctoral Fellows gone on to teach in church-related colleges and universities—including those within the LFP National

iv

Network—but many have now attained positions of leadership on their campuses, within the LFP, and within the larger conversation regarding church-related higher education. Several former post-doctoral Fellows have served as campus representatives for LFP Network Schools or on the LFP National Network Board, and others have seen their own students enter the Lilly Graduate Fellows Program.

In the summer of 2007, with the support of Lilly Endowment Inc., the LFP sponsored a conference to celebrate the leadership of those who had passed through the Postdoctoral Fellows Program at Valparaiso University by bringing together former Postdoctoral and Senior Fellows for a series of conversations connecting Christianity and the Academic Vocation. For three days in June 2007, on the campus of Indiana University Purdue University at Indianapolis (IUPUI), approximately seventy participants, including the LFP National Board, engaged in fellowship and conversation around four topics. The panel topics and presenters included the following:

The Christian Academic and the Public Square, with papers by former postdoctoral Fellows Jeff Zalar (University of Wisconsin-Whitewater, History), Colleen Seguin (Valparaiso University, History), James Kennedy (Free University of Amsterdam, History), and Tal Howard (Gordon College, History);

The Christian Academic at Home: Finding the Balance, with papers by former postdoctoral Fellows Jeremy Day-O'Connell (Knox College, Music), Lisa DeBoer (Westmont College, Art), Peter Mercer-Taylor (University of Minnesota, Music) and Stephanie Yuhl (College of the Holy Cross, History);

The Christian Academic and the Professional Guild, with papers by former postdoctoral Fellows Paul Harvey (University of Colorado-Colorado

Springs, History), Maria LaMonaca (Columbia College, English), Heath White (University of North Carolina-Wilmington, Philosophy), and J. Michael Utzinger (Hampden-Sydney College, Religion); and

The Christian Academic and the Church, with papers by former postdoctoral Fellows Kathleen Sprows Cummings (University of Notre Dame/ Cushwa Center, History), Martha Eads (Eastern Mennonite University, English), John Fea (Messiah College, History), and Scott Huelin (Union University, Humanities).

All those involved in the conference came away not only with a strong sense of the maturity and contribution of the Fellows and the LFP itself, but also with a deep appreciation for the beauty of transformational human relationships.

The papers collected in this volume represent a portion of those presented at the conference. Because of the personal nature of the papers on the panel "The Christian Academic and the Home," those essays have not been included. This is regretful, since this panel was revealing, engaging, and even prophetic. The essay by Mark Schwehn, Project Director of the LFP, entitled "Embracing Wisdom," served as a keynote address for the conference, and it concludes this volume.

Taken together, these papers explore the tensions Christian academics and church-related institutions face as they navigate the overlapping worlds of public discourse, academe, and Christianity. While these writers engage these tensions differently, they, like the LFP itself, refuse to fall into simple oppositional paradigms. The aims of the academy—when it follows its better angels—are good, be they defined as participating in human virtue, the virtues of thought, or the pursuit of what is good and true. Yet, as Mark Schwehn notes in *Exiles from Eden*, the activities associated with academic work—questioning, doubting, probing, discovery, mastery—are also connected to the human vices of arrogance, envy, and enmity.[1] Moreover, while the church helped give birth to the modern university, tensions like those between "faith and reason" or "religion and science" have borne bitter and destructive conflicts. All that is to say that, for a Christian scholar or church-related institution, navigating the academic enterprise requires the thoughtfulness evident in these essays.

Finally, it is appropriate that these essays combine the theoretical and the personal, since such a combination reflects the goals of the Lilly Postdoctoral Fellowship—that Fellows grow in an understanding of church-related mission generally, and of how that mission will play out in their lives specifically. Another way these essays tie together is that they grow from actual thought and practice in real places. The experiences reflected in the essays occur in a particular time at the end of the twentieth and the beginning of the twenty-first century—a period, as Thomas A. Howard's essay notes, in which plausibility structures in public and academic discourse have perhaps become more amenable to Christian presuppositions. Moreover, these experiences occur in specific places—Colorado Springs for Paul Harvey; an institution with a 4–4 teaching load for Maria LaMonaca. And they take place within certain communities—specific church communities, academic guilds, and academic departments. As place shapes practice, so does it shape the identities we forge—identities as parents, professors, teachers, scholars, Christians. Finally, these essays draw on a rich theological vocabulary to provide guidance as we navigate these tensions: dual citizenship, Christian monasticism, virtuous friendship, hospitality, and, finally, from Mark Schwehn, wisdom. Taken together, these essays epitomize the thoughtful collaboration that marks the Lilly Fellows Program.

As with all projects such as this, many people have contributed their time and energy, and I would like to acknowledge and thank them all. I would first like to extend my thanks to the panelists named above, and to those who convened the panels: Keith Egan, Lee Hardy, Mark Schwehn, and Susan VanZanten. Special thanks are given, as well, to Kathy Sutherland, Program Coordinator for the LFP, Margaret Franson, former Assistant Director of the LFP and current conference consultant, Arlin Meyer and Mel Piehl, former Program Directors of the LFP, Ann Spurgeon, former Office

Manager of the LFP, and Anne Sutherland Clarke, who assisted with the conference. Thanks indeed go to the generosity of Lilly Endowment Inc., to Valparaiso University for hosting and supporting the Lilly Fellows Program, and to Indiana University Purdue University Indianapolis for its hospitality in hosting the conference. A special thanks also to James Paul Old, who has edited this collection. Finally, I want to remember and celebrate the great life of John Steven Paul, Professor of Theater at Valparaiso University and Program Director of the LFP from 2005 until his death in 2009. John was the creative and organizational force behind this conference; he organized the sessions and developed the themes. I am pleased that he has been named co-editor of this volume, and I am also pleased that the work is dedicated to his memory.

Joe Creech
LFP Program Director
Valparaiso, Indiana
2010

Endnotes

1. Mark Schwehn, *Exiles from Eden* (New York: Oxford University Press, 1993), 132–133.

The Christian Academic and
the Public Square

CHAPTER ONE

On Plausibility, Post-Secularism, and Evangelicalism

Thomas Albert Howard

The topic "The Christian Academic and the Public Square" obviously marks off huge intellectual territory, and as a scholar, one's first temptation is to burnish one's higher-learning *bona fides* by a flurry of pedantic quibbles, questions, and qualifications. Who defines "Christian?" Is there such a thing as "*the* Christian?" Aren't there a teeming plurality of "public squares?" And so on. The game might be called the adornment of starting-block hand-wringing.

But let me sin more boldly and advance several broad observations-cum-theses about the "state of play" between Christian intellectual life and public life circa 2007. In particular, what might one say on this topic (with *more* reasonable confidence) that might not have been possible to say (or only with *less* reasonable confidence) at the time of the founding of the Lilly Fellows Program (LFP) in the early 1990s? Some of these points are surely idiosyncratic, particular to my own disciplinary-, faith-, and institutional locations, but I hope that they might nonetheless have a broader relevance, or, perhaps more importantly, elicit better-thought-out, contrapuntal responses.

To abet my bold sinning, I shall invoke the work of the distinguished sociologist of religion and culture, Peter Berger; in particular, I draw on his time-tested concept of *plausibility structure(s)*, advanced in such seminal works as *The Sacred Canopy* (1967) and *The Heretical Imperative* (1979).[1] In all-too-brief terms, "plausibility structures" refers to that ever-changing, complex tapestry of events, ideas, and institutions operative in any given society that confer plausibility on some arguments and modes of reasoning, but render others strange, exotic, or simply beyond comprehension. Newspapers of record, key peer-reviewed journals, influential public figures, and other fixtures of cultural authority all contribute to the plausibility environment at any given time. To be sure, one's ideas might be *valid* (internally) without a congenial plausibility environment, but they would not necessarily be *viable* (externally—in culture, in public space). For those like me, inclined to believe that ideas are both important and consequential, attentiveness to plausibility structures has been, and remains, an abiding component of the task of Christian thought and scholarship.

My general point, then, is this: In recent decades, because of the confluence of a number of factors, plausibility structures in American society (much less so in Europe) have moved, haltingly but surely, in a direction notably favorable to serious Christian thought and its viability (and visibility) in public life. Let me suggest, in thumbnail fashion, a few reasons why I think this to be the case—some of these reasons are largely external to the many-layered precincts of Christian thought in this country, but some are more internal to them. I shall conclude by commenting on a few possible prescriptive implications.

First and foremost, it seems not only safe these days, but downright fashionable to generalize that "secularization theory" or the "secularization thesis"—long a dominant social-scientific master narrative explaining modernity—has been decisively challenged, refuted by events (the swooning of Marxism, the resurgence of Islam, the rise of Global-South Christianity, the success of Mormonism, etc.), as well as by serious scholarship (not least by that of Peter Berger himself).[2] Although the thesis still has its insistent defenders,[3] the "melancholy, long withdrawing roar" of "the Sea of

Faith," pensively prophesied by Matthew Arnold in the nineteenth century, appears unlikely to happen any time soon. Models of human nature and modernization processes oblivious to, or dismissive of, the abiding purchase of religious faith on human thought and action seem well-positioned for a richly deserved obsolescence. I cannot express this any better than James Turner of the University of Notre Dame, so let me simply quote him:

> No serious observer can any longer cling to the old, rather smug conviction that modernization will gradually make religion fade away (even if the observer still wishes it would). The assumption that faith is a waning force, a theory inherited from Victorian agnostics and once widely shared among European and American academics, is now seen to be patently wrong as a matter of practical fact—indeed dangerously wrong in today's world. In consequence, scholars who are themselves secular in outlook are taking more interest in religion as a living force. And especially against the background of Islamicist radicalism, ultra-Orthodox Israeli nationalism, and weird Christian sects like the Branch Davidians, ordinary Christianity no longer seems so musty and atavistic. Christianity is certainly not chic in many academic circles, but neither can it be consigned to irrelevance.[4]

My second point, perhaps already adumbrated in the first, is that the decline of secularization theory (among other factors) has created a genuine curiosity and theoretical openness, conducive both to the treatment of religion as an object of inquiry, and (perhaps more haltingly) to the acceptance of religious perspectives as legitimate modes of inquiry into various subjects, including secularism itself. One could assemble a formidable cast of high-profile, trans-Atlantic public intellectuals (whether religious, irreligious, or areligious) to make this point: Jürgen Habermas, the late Richard Rorty, Gianni Vattimo, Alan Wolfe, Mark Lilla, Peter Schneider, Niall Ferguson, and many others. Perhaps it is just my perception, but it seems as if every other issue of the *Chronicle of Higher Education* in recent years has had a piece touching on the religious. Some representative titles include "The Greening of the World's Religions" (Mary Evelyn Tucker and John Grim), "America's Profound Ignorance of Religion" (Stephen Prothero), "What the West Can Learn from Islam" (Tariq Ramada), "Professors are More Religious Than Some Might Assume" (Thomas Bartlett), "Harvard Panel Proposes the Required Study of Religion" (Wilson Robin), and so on. In an essay penned by Stanley Fish for the *Chronicle*, "One University, Under God?", we find this arresting line: "When Jacques Derrida died," writes Fish, "I was called by a reporter who wanted to know what would succeed high theory and the triumvirate of race, gender, and class as the center of intellectual energy in the academy. I answered like a shot: religion."[5] To be sure, Stanley Fish is no infallible barometer of the academic *Zeitgeist*, but his considerable voice is also not beside the point.

Perhaps this emerging intellectual landscape is best summed up in the title (if not the argument) of C. John Sommerville's recent book, *The Decline of the Secular University*—a title that suggests both the past admissibility of secularization-of-the-academy arguments, but also their limitations if one is to think well and accurately about the present and future. Thanks in part to criticisms of academic secularization (and, with it, of the intellectual insularity that such thinking often breeds) and the undeniable religious vitality and complexity afoot in the world today, we have entered upon what he calls the "post secular."[6] Whether we should affirm or lament this condition I will not say, but at the very least, it appears to make more room—or has the potential to make more room—for engaged Christian thought than earlier periods of a more self-confident, if naïve, secularity.

My third thesis, more internal to the goings-on of Christian thought, is that evangelical Christians, once the self-ghettoized and ostracized stepchildren to respectable Christian thought and polite discourse, are not only in the mix now, but are increasingly shaping the tempo and direction of contemporary discussions. The evangelical exodus from the life of the mind occurred during the

Modernist-Fundamentalist debates in the early twentieth century. The excesses of fundamentalist "Christ-against-Culture" thinking (to use H. Richard Niebuhr's category) were first pointedly challenged in the postwar period by so-called "neo-evangelicals," such as Carl Henry and Harold Ockenga. Neo-evangelicals, as the story is often told, went on to find powerful intellectual sustenance in Kuyperian Neo-Calvinism. And the rest, as they say, is history. Quite literally history, as the evangelical intellectual renaissance of recent decades has born particularly notable fruit in historical scholarship—particularly American historical scholarship. Names such as Harry Stout, Mark Noll, George Marsden, D. G. Hart, Nathan Hatch, and a handful of others continue to possess a near incantatory aura in many discussions of Christianity and intellectual life—and not only in evangelical circles.[7]

In brief, then, these are my general points: plausibility structures—they are a changin'; secularization theory is routed, if not moribund; the "post secular" rears its sizeable, indistinct head in the academy (and in broader public life); and evangelicals, once aloof ne'r-do-wells of serious Christian thought, are beginning to sit in the front of the class—and even to raise their hands.

Can anything good come from this state of affairs? Is the Enlightenment project over as the God-Delusion (to use Richard Dawkins's term) lives on? What (old) beast, its hour come round at last, slouches toward Voltaire's Paris to be (re)born? Where, between the fear mongering secularist fundamentalism of Dawkins et al. and the old-fashioned religious variety, are nuanced, searching answers to these questions to be sought out? Herewith, a few thoughts by way of conclusion:

1) With respect to secularization/secularism, Christians engaged in scholarly and public discussions would do especially well now to avoid simple reductionisms. In the past, Christians have been among the most astute critics of economic reductionism, whether of the Marxist or Chicago School variety, which tended to reduce the complexity of human actions to economic motivations—ignoring culture and religion in particular. They should remember their own words and not, in turn, over-emphasize religious motivations. It is

7

good that religion is back on the public-scholarly agenda; it is also good if serious thought motivated by religious concerns or focused on religious objects assiduously seeks to situate itself in a rich and varied nexus of interdisciplinarity and candid recognition of the complexity and unpredictability of things human.

2) The cultural condition of post-secularity brings with it new dangers, certainly, but also new opportunities, especially for ecumenical communication and collaboration among those branches of Christianity that in earlier periods regarded one another with great hostility and suspicion. The significant rapprochement between some evangelicals and some Roman Catholics in this country in recent years might serve as an apt case-in-point. The cross-pollination of confessions and intellectual traditions epitomized by the Lilly Fellows Program is itself—I am inclined to think—part cause, part consequence of new possibilities. In both cases, Christians who desire to engage in broader discussions have the chance to draw from a deeper pool of theological resources than their individual traditions might allow. A multi-dimensional theological *ressourcement* is and remains afoot, I would hazard. And foundations such as the Lilly Endowment and the Pew Charitable Trust deserve much credit for helping foster this. (As I've heard one wag put it: wherever two or three Christian scholars are gathered, there is Lilly or Pew in their midst!)

3) But this *ressourcement* can and should be deepened, and perhaps pushed into more delicate and difficult areas. And here, I am speaking particularly *within* Protestantism. (Catholic readers are invited to be sympathetic eavesdroppers.) In participating in many denominationally diverse conversations, in listening to numerous celebrations of the strengths and particularities of individual institutions and traditions, in discussing the shape of Christian public engagement, one still observes a rather thick divide between, for want of better terms, "evangelical intellectuals"—those whose theological habits of comprehension and intellectual engagement have been shaped by one side of the Modernist-Fundamentalist debate—and "mainline intellectuals"—those whose theological habits of comprehension and intellectual engagement have been shaped by the other side. Admittedly, this so-called "two-party" understanding

of the Protestant landscape has been challenged well and often by scholars, but its descriptive power is not negligible, and we would do well to remember Wallace Stevens's lines, that we more often "live in the description of the place and not the place itself."[8]

One's understanding of the task and posture of the Christian public intellectual, I would submit, differs considerably based on which side of this debate one locates one's deepest theological-cum-intellectual instincts. Again in the language of H. Richard Niebuhr, the modernist camp and its far-flung progeny in contemporary Christian thought and institution-building have embodied more of a "Christ of Culture" approach to public discourse, a belief that culture (elite academic culture in particular) should shape and penetrate the task of Christian thought extensively, an approach that grants post-Enlightenment "Athens" rather extensive rights of suffrage within "Jerusalem."

Conversely, evangelicals and their scholarly venues and institutions have embodied and brought to expression more of a Tertullianist, *contra-mundum* "Christ against Culture" approach, whereby culture is viewed rather suspiciously, as something to be separated from (in the more purist Tertullianist varieties), or in the more Calvinist-Kuyperian strands of evangelicalism, as something to be understood in order to be reformed—Christ transforming Culture.[9]

I suppose, then, my concluding question is this: Can thoughtful people shaped by both camps—"Christ against Culture" and "Christ of Culture"—be prompted to speak to one another, not only about their many commonalities, but also about their deepest differences for the purpose of a greater common good; for Christian public engagement; and not least, though most vexingly difficult of all, for ecclesiastical unity? It seems as if the "Christ against Culture" and "Christ of Culture" models of engagement possess not only antithetical, but also (potentially) *mutually correcting and self-clarifying principles*. If unchecked, Christ-against-Culture leads to an overweening sense of righteousness and separatist insularity, and the Christian intellectual in this environment ends up, all too often, preaching to the choir. Conversely, if unchecked, the Christ-of-Culture model leads to an all-too-complacent accommodation of mainstream intellectual culture—and, as many mainline enterprises know too well, to the possibility of no longer having a choir to preach to! Continuing to figure out how to move, however ploddingly, from antithetical assessments to ones that stress the mutually correcting and self-clarifying seems, in the final analysis, not an unimportant item for Christian intellectual life, for the sake of public expression, to be sure, but perhaps for deeper purposes as well.

Endnotes

1. Peter Berger, *The Sacred Canopy: Elements of a Sociological Theory of Religion* (Garden City, New York: Doubleday, 1967) and *The Heretical Imperative: Contemporary Possibilities of Religious Affirmation* (Garden City, New York: Anchor Press, 1979).

2. Cf. Peter Berger, ed., *The Desecularization of the World: Resurgent Religion and World Politics* (Grand Rapids: Eerdmans, 1999).

3. See, e.g., Steve Bruce, *God is Dead: Secularization in the West* (Oxford: Blackwell, 2002).

4. Mark Noll and James Turner, *The Future of Christian Learning: An Evangelical and Catholic Dialogue*, ed. Thomas Albert Howard (Grand Rapids: Brazos Press, 2008).

5. Stanley Fish, "One University, under God?" *The Chronicle of Higher Education* (January 7, 2005): C4.

6. C. John Sommerville, *The Decline of the Secular University* (Oxford, 2006). Cf. Michael Novak, "Remembering the Secular Age," *First Things* No. 174 (2007): 35–40.

7. See Alan Wolfe, "The Opening of the Evangelical Mind," *Atlantic Monthly* 286 (October 2000): 55 ff; also see James Turner, "Something to be Reckoned with: The Evangelical Mind Awakens," *Commonweal* Vol. 126, No. 1 (January 15, 1999): 11–23.

8. In this paragraph, I draw from Douglas Jacobsen and Willian Vance Trollinger Jr., "Evangelical and Ecumenical: Re-Forming a Center," *Christian Century* 111 (July 13, 1994): 682(3).

9. On the terminology, see H. Richard Niebuhr, *Christ and Culture* (San Francisco: HarperCollins, 1996), 45ff., 83ff., 190ff.

CHAPTER TWO

The Roots of Public Virtue in Christian Intellectual Practice

Jeffrey T. Zalar

"The Christian Academic in the Public Square" is a topic that I'm not sure I should be addressing. I'm afraid I don't have any stunning or settled views to share on it, not because I do not ponder the proper role Christian academics ought to play in public—I do, and frequently—but because I have no experience of a public academic life to draw upon for insights. I teach courses in the public spaces of my university, and I address peers at the public meetings of my discipline, but I spend the rest of my time alone in private study, attempting to make sense of modern European history. And isn't this the way with most of us in the academy most of the time? Whether publishing or, I contend, teaching, our primary and absorbing activity is, or should be, private study. If, then, we are going to assert right orientations for how we behave in public life, we ought to begin by considering how we order our private lives of study.

Now, the paradigmatic practices of learning in the Christian tradition are monastic. We should not resist the pull of this anach-ronism. Otherwise, we might forget long-held attitudes toward knowledge and its possession, and proven methods that lend our learning purpose, and so build our house on sand. Despite its reputation for detachment from the world, monastic culture aimed to generate publicly relevant knowledge among individuals whose contemplative routines made them uniquely available to their neighbors. The monastic style, in other words, is not an outdated prescription, but a distinctive mode of study and religious dedication that can enable our learning to obtain its fullest significance. Most importantly, monastic culture enlarges the heart, mitigating the danger a scholar always poses to communal life, which is *to divide*.

Please allow me to explain. I declare that no specimen of the human race is more capable of exhibiting the virtue of friendship than a scholar. This is because a scholar's natural love—our natural love, the kind of love most pertinent to our calling—is *philia*, or a preferential love for particular objects and individuals. Ivan Illich will support me on this point. In his delightful commentary on Hugh of St. Victor, Illich observes that study is a deep concept, one whose historic meanings drive down to affection for privileged things, friendliness, and devotion to another's welfare.[1] By this thick understanding, study implies more than the banal accumulation of facts and their arrangement into plausible views of the phenomenal world by disembodied, "austere" individuals.[2] Rather, it involves entire thinking subjects as enfleshed intellectual souls, whose flourishing as knowers and full dignity as persons depend upon their active inclusion in the broadest possible communities. The redoubtable A. G. Sertillanges, for all his insistence on the merits of solitude, agrees with his usual gusto, declaring study to be a "kinship of minds," whose cooperative spirit "draws out our richest and deepest resources; it unfolds the wings of our dreams and hidden indeterminate thoughts; it serves as a check on our judgments, tries out our new ideas, keeps up our ardor, and inflames our enthusiasm." Such is the "obstetric art" of friendship, without which the scholar becomes "timid, abstracted, a little odd."[3]

In all events, we know from our own experience that we have a ravenous appetite for the items of our attraction, as well as for those individuals—a mentor, a leader in our field who encourages our career, a star student, a co-author—who share our passion, and with whom we constitute an exclusive community of interest.

This penchant for philia pervades our scholarly lives. A grammarian is a logophile. Biologists who love birds are ornithophiles. One who studies Central Europe like me is a Germanophile. We are all bibliophiles. Philia expresses itself epistemologically in our preference for the part over the whole, organizationally in the taxonomy of disciplinary specializations, affectively in the "schools of thought" to which we belong, and procedurally in our inclination to sort, split, and cut: sociological typecasting, philological genealogy, crop splicing and hybridity, atomic bombardment, autopsy.

I believe that this penchant for philia is our distinctive excellence as productive men and women, and therefore, it is the source of the best we have to offer civilized life. Our abilities to define problems and propose apposite solutions, to equip society with innovative instruments, and to raise questions that preserve and challenge culture, along with the counterbalance our learned opinions exert on the views of the collective and our cosmopolitanism's leverage against narrow parochial tastes—all of these attributes of elevated and enhanced public life stem from our honorable predilection toward philia.

Not surprisingly, as scholars themselves, the medieval monks were enthusiastic about philia's relationship to a suggestive life of the mind. "He cannot take up the plow?" Peter the Venerable asked in the twelfth century,

> Then let him take up the pen; it is much more useful.
> In the furrows he traces on the parchment, he will
> sow the seeds of the divine words ... He will preach
> without opening his mouth; without breaking silence,
> he will make the Lord's teaching resound in the ears
> of the nations; and without leaving his cloister, he
> will journey far over land and sea.[4]

The monks, in fact, transposed pagan philia into Christian culture not only by their commentaries on cherished texts, but by all of their work in the ensemble of medieval scholarship, which sprang from an abiding esteem for erudition: their preservation of classical memory; their love of language and orthography; their study of the ancient naturalists; their expository writing on the Latin Bible; their promotion of the liberal arts; their copying, rubricating, painting, calligraphy, and bookbinding in the *Scriptorium*. The end of these activities might have been love of God, but their everyday élan, and the driving force of the humanism that produced them, was philia. Let us listen to Smaragdus, the abbot of Saint Mihiel during the Carolingian revival of the ninth century, as he sings the praises of grammar:

> Here you will find that measure of gold which comes from Heaven and which we have been accorded by the Holy Spirit Himself ... This little book is full of holy gifts; it contains Scripture and it is seasoned with grammar. Scripture teaches us to seek after the kingdom of God, to detach the self from the earth, to rise above the self. It promises the blessed ... to live with the Lord [and] to dwell always with Him. Grammar, then, through the goodness of God, confers great benefits on those who read it with care.[5]

As we can see, for Smaragdus, grammar was not just a discipline of the mind, but an object of friendship which led individuals to heaven by eliciting from them a full and fine quality of their souls. This intimate coordination among philia, study, and public relevance was brought forward into modern times by the Renaissance Humanists. Thomas More's carefully regulated life of study drew its inspiration from his years among Carthusian monks at Charterhouse in London. And while Erasmus may have developed "a permanent distaste for monastic life" after spending nearly a decade as an Augustinian canon, as a result of his cloistering, he could still say that, in the end, books were his best friends.[6]

Now, this is all very good, and we are celebrating the academic's ability to make friends. But wait: everyone can make a friend. Friendship is a practice of the saint as well as the snob. That truth is the special virtue of optimists, who insist that, even without them, all good things are possible; it is the special vice of debunkers, who insist that, without them, no good things are possible. Friendship can emancipate; it can also imprison. It might declare, "I have a dream"; it might build a Gulag.

The problem is with philia's inherent selfishness. Because, by its nature, friendship is preferential love, it invites us to love those who share our attractions, but it imposes no duty to love those who do not, and this is why a scholar, blessed with a singular aptitude for friendship, is always a loaded cannon in the public square. Our friendship might seek the good of all, and this is the best kind of friendship, as Aristotle remarked in the *Ethics*.[7] But it might just as easily seek only what is useful and pleasurable to our group, and with a power to distract, deceive, corrupt, and control those outside it, that is truly terrifying. So easily can the goodness of our *furor amicus* degenerate into a rough *furor politicus*, which does not integrate and uplift, but excludes and estranges. And what manner of mischief has not been loosed upon the world as a result? We are all familiar with the consequences: falsehood and delusion in public discourse; Balkanization of common life on the basis of adamant truth claims; the mobilization of people to violence in the service of dubious and overwrought ideas; "the despotic and Jacobin ruthlessness of the pure of heart," who tell the wretched people that they lead, "you will be happy and good, whether you want to or not."[8] And in avoiding this wickedness, this "treason of the intellectuals," as Julien Benda famously put it, let us not place too much store in our Christian conviction.[9] Friendship, C. S. Lewis reminds us, for all its merits, divides.[10] How many times have we seen it and been ashamed? How many times have cliques of Christians, full of faith and full of themselves, made the Gospel say what it does not say in order to satisfy the desires of friendly faction? *"Exsurge domine et vindica causam* nostram!*"* St. Paul had something to say about this: "I urge you brothers to watch out for those who create divisions and obstacles in opposition to the teaching that you learned; avoid them. For such people do not serve our Lord Christ but their own appetites, and by fair and flattering speech they deceive the hearts of the innocent" (Romans 16: 17–18).

Now, this is all very bad, and we are lamenting our ability to make friends. But hold once again: There is something remarkable buried deep within monastic culture. Here, we find that, on the one hand, as exemplars of philia, the monks more than anyone in Christian culture upheld the virtues of exclusive love.[11] But in the same sources, we find that, in the ancient and medieval worlds, the monks were also exemplars of *agape*, that most especial form of inclusive love, which is neither selfish nor preferential, but generous-hearted, even toward enemies. The monks studied, but they also saved souls. They took up positions in an interpretive community, but they also took in strangers. They argued in full throat, but with equal zeal, they welcomed visitors and gave alms. They lived in seclusion, and yet everyone who lived on their grounds was considered part of their family.[12] The monks, in other words, cultivated a disposition toward others in which the natural friendliness of scholarship remained as it was, and yet it was completed as a mode of charity large enough to love adversaries as much as allies, aliens as fervently as the most familiar companions. And how did they accomplish this feat? I believe the answer lies in the concrete patterns of their contemplative prayer.

I wonder if Christian higher education initiatives in general, and the Lilly Fellows Program in particular, have taken the connection between study and prayer seriously enough. Discussions of the integration of faith and learning usually turn on mission maintenance at the institutional level, and on such academic activities at the programmatic level as teaching, mentorship, and the development of sub-societies on campus which anchor the university's learning community and elaborate its ethos. But these discussions, however vital, are insufficient to define a Christian university, and they do not exhaust a Christian scholar's responsibilities. What we do in private, in the quiet and repose of our studies, is just as, if not more, foundational to the life of the mind as the public activities I have mentioned. I suggest that, in order to advance the agenda of Christian higher education, we must ground our scholarship, too, in the rich traditions of Christian faith by investigating the transcendent backing of the intellectual life and engendering the practices that sustain it.[13]

A central observance of such a life is contemplative prayer. I benefited in many ways from the Lilly Fellows Program, but no development in me has been of more lasting significance than my adoption, with Mark Schwehn, of a daily prayer discipline. I could scarcely have realized it then, but Mark was introducing me to a practice of tremendous value for Christian intellectuals active in the public square. Cloistered monks have much to teach us. The defining characteristic of their culture was regular contemplation, and contemplation implied the self-transcendence achieved especially through *lectio divina* and meditation on the Holy Word, which facilitated their daily encounters with the sacred. And although much of this prayer occurred in withdrawal from others and along a vector of intention which was primarily vertical, it also opened the monks to the world around them by transforming all they did, including study, into a perpetual quest for holiness. Contemplative self-transcendence alone eroded friendly selfishness.[14] The silence of contemplation that enabled the monks to hear God sharpened their receptivity to hear others, too, and not just their friends, but everyone with whom they sought to live in organic unity. In hearing God, the monks were made aware of their great need of God, and this sense of helplessness built in them an abiding humility which tempered all pride in themselves and their groups. By focusing so intensely on Heaven, they encountered the Sovereign Creator of life and all knowledge about it. In awe of this Creator, they judged what they learned not by the inherent characteristics of an isolated part, but, as Jean LeClercq once put it, "in relationship with the final consummation of the whole of reality."[15] Their "friendly" pursuit of knowledge, then, could never end in arrogant secession, indifference, casuistry, callousness, oppression, or violence; it could only end in an embracing beatitude of all in all.

We Christian academics must do and say in the public square what our vocations call us to do and say, and this is to offer specialized knowledge for public improvement. Our disposition toward philia is a lamp which must not be dampened because of its potential to burn. But let us intensify its light with the radiance of charity, remembering the words of Saint Anthony, the founder of Western monasticism, when he said that, despite all insularity appropriate to our calling, "Our life and death is with our neighbor."

I would like to conclude with a prayer for monastic life endorsed by the Alliance for International Monasticism:

O loving God, we ask your blessing on all monastic men and women … Help them to become people of prayer and peace. May they be visible signs that strangers can live together in God's love. Give them hearts wide enough to welcome the traveler, the outcast, the neighbor. Enable them to listen to and learn from the people they serve, especially the poorest. May their communities be models of wise stewardship, of dignified human labor, of sacred leisure, and of reverence for all living things. Above all, O God, may a monastic presence in the world be a constant witness of justice, compassion and hope to all. Amen.[16]

Endnotes

1. Ivan Illich, *In the Vineyard of the Text: A Commentary to Hugh's* Didascalicon (Chicago: The University of Chicago Press, 1993), p. 14. On pp. 26–8, Illich relates Hugh's conviction that friendship, as a derivative of the "love of wisdom," was the motivating force behind reading.

2. On austerity in modern intellectual life, see Mark R. Schwehn, *Exiles from Eden: Religion and the Academic Vocation in America* (New York: Oxford University Press, 1993), pp. 8–9.

3. A. G. Sertillanges, O. P., *The Intellectual Life: Its Spirit, Conditions, Methods*, trans. Mary Ryan (Washington, DC: The Catholic University of America Press, 1998), pp. 53–61, here pp. 56 and 59.

4. Quoted in Jean LeClercq, O.S.B., *The Love of Learning and the Desire for God* (New York: Fordham University Press, 2003), p. 123.

5. Quoted in LeClercq, p. 44.

6. Peter Ackroyd, *The Life of Thomas More* (New York: Random House, 1998), p. 82.

7. *Nicomachean Ethics,* 1157a, 18–21. For the rest of this section, see C. S. Lewis, *The Four Loves* (New York: Harcourt, 1988), pp. 57–90; Gilbert Meilaender, *Friendship: A Study in Theological Ethics* (Notre Dame, IN: University

of Notre Dame Press, 1980), pp. 6–35; and Paul J. Wadell, C.P., *Friendship and the Moral Life* (Notre Dame, IN: University of Notre Dame Press, 1989), pp. 70–119.

8. This is a paraphrase of Peter Gay in *Mozart: A Penguin Life* (New York: Penguin, 1999), p. 85.

9. Julien Benda, *La trahison des clercs* (Paris: B. Grasset, 1927).

10. Lewis, p. 86.

11. Meilaender, p. 1. We are discussing here the intimate unity of intellectual and moral virtues, a topic analyzed with precision by Linda Trinkaus Zagzebski in *Virtues of the Mind: An Inquiry into the Nature of Virtue and the Ethical Foundations of Knowledge* (New York: Cambridge University Press, 1996).

12. See Christine D. Pohl, *Making Room: Recovering Hospitality as a Christian Tradition* (Grand Rapids, MI: Eerdmans, 1999), pp. 46–51. New work in the historiography of western monasticism insists that its practices were simultaneously contemplative and active. See, for example, Sarah Foot, *Monastic Life in Anglo-Saxon England, c. 600-900* (New York: Cambridge University Press, 2006).

13. A step in this direction is James W. Sire, *Habits of the Mind: Intellectual Life as a Christian Calling* (Downers Grove, IL: InterVarsity Press, 2000).

14. Josef Pieper, whose perspective was steeped in monastic traditions, draws the connection between contemplative love of God and selfless love of others in *Glück und Kontemplation* (Munich: Kösel-Verlag, 1979), pp. 70–74.

15. LeClercq, p. 66.

16. Judith Sutera, O.S.B., ed., *Work of God: Benedictine Prayer*, (Collegeville, MN: The Liturgical Press, 1997), p. 105.

CHAPTER THREE

Classrooms as Public Squares

Colleen Seguin

We have been given the charge to reflect on the question, "What responsibilities does the Christian academic bear for addressing issues and concerns of audiences beyond the classroom and the campus, in the city, the region, the state, and the nation?" I will frankly admit that this charge initially worried me greatly. I am not a letter to the editor or op-ed writer; I am not a public intellectual; I am not the most famous man in the Netherlands; I am not part of any political activist organizations; I do not volunteer for any organizations; I have never incorporated service learning into my courses; and I don't practice "relevant" scholarship.

By "relevant," I mean timely—ripped straight from the headlines-stuff. I don't teach those sorts of things, and I don't research those sorts of things. I am an early modernist, and I work on Englishwomen and the social history of Catholicism—plenty important to me, I assure you, but unlikely to inspire an episode of *Law and Order*. In contrast, I have a colleague at Valparaiso University who taught a history of immigration class this semester, is involved in local initiatives to aid immigrants, has spoken at pro-immigrant rallies, is teaching a course on the history of homelessness in the fall, and has had a long relationship with both the campus's and the city's chapters of Habitat for Humanity. That kind of cross-fertilization between the academic and the "public" is something I admire deeply, but not something that I practice; it's not my vocation.

So, indeed, why am I here? I may have persuaded you, as well, that I'm not the public square type. But I do teach, and teaching does have public relevance, no matter what your subject matter (although the public relevance is, of course, more apparent in teaching say, evolutionary biology at a conservative university, versus teaching about the roles of women in early modern Catholicism). Thus, although our charge asked us to reflect on our responsibilities for developing relationships to audiences *beyond* the classroom, and on the resources within Christian traditions to assist in such endeavors, I would argue that: 1) developing those relationships through what happens *in* the classroom occurs more than we might imagine, and 2) the relationships within the classroom itself are of vitally important civic significance, too, if one takes seriously, as teachers (especially Christian ones) should, the formation of ethical citizens as part of a pedagogical vocation.[1] As the sociologist Eleanor Townsley states, rather than viewing a campus as an "alternative universe," we should understand it as "a very important public sphere" possessing "community dynamics that are consequential."[2]

So how does what occurs in class connect to what we might, for convenience's sake, call the classroom's "constituencies" beyond the students sitting there in front of you every day? As we all know, the classroom is not, nor should it be, just an extension of our offices, or our studies, or a monastic cell, into which we admit larger numbers of people than those spaces could feasibly accommodate. Rather, as a community that we forge with our students day-in and day-out, the classroom is, at least in part, a forum for communicating with a variety of constituencies (this list is not exhaustive, but it is what I'll focus on). Students, of course, are the primary audience, but for the purpose of this paper, I won't assess them on their own. Rather, I'll analyze their role as conduits to the constituencies of: a) parents and b) churches. And then there's constituency c)—for which I am primarily the conduit in my courses—dead people. (This is discipline-specific to some extent, but what I mean here is one's subject matter.) Constituency c) is beyond the scope of my discussion today, but it is worth noting that there are times when one does need to plead with students to simply "read" a discipline on its own terms, not solely in terms of its personal connection to them.

Parents are part of every class; they are always there, albeit invisibly. One of my graduate school mentors was fond of saying that, in fact, particularly when you teach first-year students, you are really teaching their parents. Generally speaking, that is who they are at that point in their development. Of course parents, these ever-present "shadow students," are not invisible when one works with Admissions, meeting with parents of prospective students and having to answer the classic, "But what can she *do* with a history major??" question. Not surprisingly, a recent survey from the Association of American Colleges and Universities examining why students attend college notes that "students consider the least important outcomes of a college education [to be] values and ethics, an appreciation of cultural diversity, global awareness, and civic responsibility." These students believe "that college is important to their success in the work force, but they do not recognize its role in preparing them as citizens, community participants, and thoughtful people."[3] Clearly such concerns are not solely those of students; parental influences—and anxieties—are of paramount importance here. Those concerns, too, are always present, acknowledged or not, in the classroom.

Furthermore (on a different note), many of my students are clearly engaged in cell phone conversations with their parents right before my class, and then right after it, too, so it certainly seems conceivable that what happened in the class comes up. I know, likewise, that some students give their parents course texts to read at times if they think that they will find them compelling, which is another way that parents are included in the class. We all know the fashionable term for referring to the current college generation's parents is "helicopter parents," for those who are always hovering. And in my experience, that is an accurate assessment. I had my first-ever experience last fall of an advisee coming to fix her problematic first-semester schedule and inviting me to discuss the minutia of said schedule with her dad on her cell phone. I am actually glad that I did that. Hearing a parent expound upon about what a gifted foreign language student he had been in college and ponder how inexplicable it was to him, therefore, that his daughter had a pathological fear of taking Spanish taught me a lot about my advisee very rapidly. So parents are there. They are part of our public; they are rating our job performance; they are trying to decide if they are getting their "money's worth." Sometimes, they are enabling their children when they call to intercede with a faculty member who has accused a definitely guilty student of an Honor Code violation; sometimes, they write us letters thanking us for all that we have done for their children; and very significantly, in families that talk to one another, they are, at times, in essence, taking our classes at one remove.

But here are three more concrete scenarios from teaching courses on "Europe in the Age of Reformations" and "Gender, Spirituality, and Power: European Women, 1400–1700" over the years. These examples demonstrate how parents as a constituency can meld into churches as a constituency.

Anecdote 1. Reformation class: A heated classroom debate erupts over infant baptism and the controversy around that issue among different Reformation-era people. This led to a private conversation with a student as to what he was going to do about the fact that he believed in infant baptism, but his girlfriend did not. Because of my class, he at least now understood why she thought what she did, even though he still did not agree with her. But he thought that he was probably going to marry her: What would his parents and pastor say if his babies might end up not being baptized? Thus, the course gave him the tools that he needed to better understand his girlfriend's perspective, but could not prevent potential future dissent.

Anecdote 2. Reformation class: Luther and the Jews; obviously a sensitive issue at a Lutheran university. We read Luther's writings, some secondary sources, and the Lutheran Church-Missouri Synod's and the Evangelical Lutheran Church in America's modern statements on the topic. This was a balanced and nuanced treatment, I would argue. And then the calls to parents and pastors fly. Those are classroom conversations that definitely engage students' wider publics. Some students are angry at their Sunday school teachers and parents. How could this have never come up? Others immediately assume that Luther never said anything negative about the Jews at all, and that a call home or to their pastor will surely clear things up. These are difficult and important conversations to have, and they are jumpstarted by something that occurs within the not-so-private confines of a university classroom, and I am sure that all of you have multiple similar examples. Such conversations are opportunities to carefully assess the significance of the past; to reflect on definitions of "heroism"; to ponder the blind spots of certain eras, including our own; and certainly, at a church-related institution, to discuss what it means to develop an adult faith.

Anecdote 3. Women and Religion class: I have taught Linda Lierheimer's article "Preaching or Teaching?: Defining the Ursuline Mission in Seventeenth-Century France" and Margaret Fell Fox's "Women's Preaching Justified."[4] This is not material likely to end up on the big screen or the evening news, but from the perspective of Christian students at a Christian school, it is quite engaging and "relevant." One student noted that, if members of many churches were to read these pieces, they would be astonished that controversies over women's roles in church were not "invented in the 1960s." Historicizing contemporary religious debates within the classroom matters within congregations. Will this deeply pious, bright, and outspoken student remain silent in the future when those around him assert the novelty of "PC" claims for greater airing of female voices, or will those old college Xeroxes animate him? Stay tuned...

So, having assessed, fleetingly, how relationships to parental and ecclesiastical constituencies are developed through what happens within the classroom, I want to reflect briefly on how the seemingly insular relationships *within* the classroom, both among students and among teacher and students, have vital importance for civic and public discourse. It is no surprise to anyone teaching college students today that basic civility is on the decline. And, of course, it "always" has been; every older generation thinks so. Regardless of whether or not one thinks that "kids nowadays" are exceptionally irreverent and vulgar, which is probably an absurd contention, twenty-first-century public discourse is undeniably in a particularly sorry state. This presents a troubling scenario: How

25

do students find models for how to contribute to such discourse themselves, when the older adults around them are failing at it so spectacularly? The Civic Health Index of the National Conference on Citizenship provides much evidence that public life is in decline. Through analysis of forty indicators over the past thirty years, the index depicts the United States as a divisive and distrustful "nation of spectators."[5]

The chronic substitution of cleverness for wisdom in public debate is nothing new, nor is the substitution of soundbites for analysis. But the "gotcha" nature of most modern journalism and political campaigns, along with our society's obsession with the "real" ("reality" TV) and utter inability to discern the authentic, breeds a profound apathy in many students about public life. Everything's a joke; everyone's a smartass; the smartest ass wins (e.g., Bart Simpson). Within this context, emphasizing and clarifying basic elements of acceptable classroom decorum—because one can really take nothing for granted on this score—can play an important role in modeling for students what it means to be an active, discerning, civilized, informed, courteous participant in civic life. This is no small thing. As Peter Levine, executive director of the Center for Information and Research on Civic Learning and Engagement, notes, "we don't even know how to talk publicly in groups anymore."[6]

So, how does the classroom serve as a nexus for the formation of ethical citizens, keeping in mind that the average student considers ethics and values to be irrelevant parts of their higher education? It is a nexus in many ways that render classrooms important public spaces. In the classroom, students encounter a number of behaviors that are relevant to public and civic discourse: discussing ideas like they matter, like the stakes are genuine and high; ordering cell phones off and brains on; really, really listening to others, respecting them, and forbidding their interruption; democratizing classrooms to teach students to assume responsibility for class discussion (among other things), and to prepare them for the demands of democratic citizenship; trying to eliminate the phenomenon in larger classes that you, the instructor, are on television, and that they are viewers invisible to the talking head, free to chat with their fellow viewers, pass snacks around, leave for bathroom breaks five minutes into class, flip on their computers, or pull out other classes' readings if you bore them.[7] These things are not small potatoes classroom management issues; they are about helping students to develop what Simone Weil would have called a capacity for "attention." For Weil, such a concept was also, of course, about finding God even in the tedium of "school studies," even if one were to do one's math problems, for example, incorrectly. Teaching students to pay attention is not just about social control; rightly conceived of, it is about teaching them to develop the discipline and focus necessary to become attentive, decent, ethical members of a community, contributing citizens—as participants and as listeners—both in and out of classrooms. Weil noted that, "Not only does the love of God have attention for its substance; the love of our neighbor ... is made of this same substance. Those who are unhappy have no need for anything in this world but people capable of giving them their attention."[8] Likewise, "the love of our neighbor in all its fullness simply means being able to say to him [sic]: 'What are you going through?'"[9] Ideally, in classrooms of the attentive, the content of scholarly conversation, its "leakage" to the outside world, and the approach to discussion itself can help to cultivate ethical citizenship in the public square.

Endnotes

1. My thinking on the importance of teaching ethical citizenship is heavily indebted to Alan Bloom, "Civic Engagement: Teaching Ethical Citizenship in the Classroom," *Fraser Valley Research Review* Vol. 2, No. 1 (Fall, 2008): pp. 54–65.

2. "Endowment Cultivates Great Teachers," Supplement to the *Mount Holyoke Alumnae Quarterly* Vol. 91, No. 1 (Spring 2007): p. 8.

3. Carol Geary Schneider and Debra Humphreys, "Putting Liberal Education on the Radar Screen," *The Chronicle of Higher Education*, September 23, 2005, p. B20.

4. Lierheimer, in Beverly Mayne Kienzle and Pamela J. Walker, eds. *Women Preachers and Prophets through Two Millennia of Christianity* (Berkeley, CA: University of California Press, 1998), pp. 212–226; Kate Aughterson, ed.

Renaissance Woman: Constructions of Femininity in England: A Sourcebook (New York: Routledge, 1995), pp. 37–40.

5. *Broken Engagement* (Washington, DC: National Conference on Citizenship, 2006), pp. 4–5. See also Bloom's discussion of this issue, p. 54.

6. Cynthia M. Gibson, *Citizens at the Center: A New Approach to Civic Engagement* (Washington, DC: The Case Foundation, 2006), p. 22.

7. On democratizing classrooms as preparation for the demands of democratic citizenship, see Bloom, pp. 57–59.

8. Simone Weil, *Waiting for God* (New York: Perennial Classics, 2001), p. 64.

9. Weil, p. 64.

The Christian Academic and
the Academic Guild

CHAPTER FOUR

Exile from Valpo

On Being a Religious Scholar in the Historical
Guild at the Public University Amidst a Charged
Atmosphere of Religion, Politics, and War

Paul Harvey

D uring my tenure as a Lilly Fellow, I never quite thought
of Athens, Jerusalem, and Colorado Springs in the same
breath, or as part of some kind of intellectual triad. Now,
as a tenured faculty member at the University of Colorado at Colorado Springs, I do, and I'd like to explore why and think about how
Athens and Jerusalem intersect in the public square of a university
in the midst of a highly charged atmosphere of religion, politics,
and war.

Obviously, the Lilly Fellows Program explores issues
involving church-related higher education, and it is indeed at
church-related institutions where many graduates of the program
end up. On the other hand, the job market is what it is, and the vaga-
ries of life are what they are, and only God knows where we will
end up and how we will go about doing what we end up doing. In
my own case, after several frustrating years on the historical meat
market, I stumbled accidentally and fortuitously into my present
position, at the University of Colorado at Colorado Springs. Whatever else I had envisioned for my academic life before, it generally
had not included teaching classes at a university established only

during the 1960s, mostly at the behest of Hewlett-Packard executives who were demanding an engineering training school in exchange for establishing a plant in town. It had not included teaching classes now full of students ranging from eighteen to sixty-five years of age, many of whom come in full fatigue gear straight from counter-insurgency training exercises at Fort Carson or one of the other local military outposts. It had not included classes full of forty-something women who may come or not, depending on whether the babysitter shows up, or whether the kid throws a tantrum because the mother has to miss yet another T-ball game. It had not included teaching my Civil War class to students who easily compared their own post-Iraq PTSD experiences with those of the soldiers from Chancellorsville or Cold Harbor or Antietam that they were reading about. My graduate school professors at Berkeley were great teachers, but they could not have prepared me for the non-traditional classroom, as I think they scarcely knew such things existed.

And while at Valparaiso, it did not occur to me that a great number of my students for a substantial portion of my career so far would be thinking not of Athens, or of Jerusalem, or even of Aspen or the Sigma Chi party, but rather of Belgrade, Baghdad, and Fallujah; and not of the Southern Baptists, the Presbyterian Church of the United States, or of Missouri Synod Lutheranism, but instead of Focus on the Family and New Life Church.

By contrast, my training at Valparaiso had compelled me to think about the meaning of my interest and my faith within the context of a largely secularist academy, and perhaps even to prepare for battle to defend my chosen course of academic study and my faith. As it turns out, those have been the least of my worries, for reasons I'll discuss below. More troubling to me has been the devaluing of our guilds, and of higher education generally, in public discourse, as well as the increasing implication that scholarship is just so much spin that can be put on par with any other subject. Thus, I rise today not to bury my guild, nor to point out its shortcomings, but mostly to defend it, and to suggest (perhaps heretically) that the discipline of history has been reasonably non-hostile terrain for scholars of faith, or even just for scholars who *study* faith.

I also want to consider my rather peculiar position in thinking about the meeting of Athens and Jerusalem in the context of Colorado Springs, where students at a public university tend, on the whole, to be more self-consciously religious (or anti-religious), or obsessed with religious questions, than students I have encountered at church-related schools. I make no claim for typicality, but rather, I just want to think out loud about how my experiences as a Lilly Fellow have informed my current position at a public university in a city nationally know for being a center of particular brands of religious thought and practice, namely, the religious/political right and the megachurch phenomenon.

I lucked into my present position at a particularly interesting and fruitful time. For one thing, I was just concluding a two-year stint in the Young Scholars in American Religion program run out of Indiana University-Purdue University Indianapolis. For another, I had just completed my first book, on black and white Southern Baptists in the post-Civil War South, and I was beginning serious work on what later became my second book, *Freedom's Coming: Religious Cultures and the Shaping of the South from the Civil War through the Civil Rights Era.*[1] As well, I was working with the historian Philip Goff, now director of the Center for the Study of Religion and American Culture at IUPUI, on a textbook for American religious history consisting of thematic essays, now published as *Themes in Religion and American Culture.*

For another, I had the good fortune of moving into American religious history as a primary field—as much by accident as by intent, since my original interest was the history of the South and race relations in American history—just at the time when American religious history was exploding as a field. At one time, it could be said, with some justification, that American religious history was understudied and not given its due respect. Some older scholars in the field still contend that is the case, but I think they are wrong, thanks in part to a generous infusion of grant money, and also to a generation of talented historians—including older stars of the field who came up through church-related schools, such as Mark Noll, Edith Blumhofer, George Marsden, and former Lilly Fellow John McGreevy, as well as younger stars, such as my younger fellow fellows John Fea and Darren Dochuk—whose work simply commanded respect and attention.

As well, the social history revolution—not by intent, to be sure, but more by accident—propelled a renewed interest in religious history in America. Once it became doctrine that the lives of ordinary people—workers, slaves, farm women, and others—were to be taken seriously, and once historians began doing that in earnest, they discovered, of course, that religion, most especially of democratic and evangelical varieties, was foundational to the ways Americans conceived of and directed their lives, thoughts, political movements, migrations, diary entries, and emotions. This was even more the case when examining the histories of understudied ethnic groups—African Americans, Native Americans, Latinos, and others—whose stories began to be recaptured and reinterpreted in light of the social movements of the 1960s.

To be sure, the revolution of taking religion seriously in the guild of history did not start with this generation; Perry Miller had done it much earlier with the Puritans. And, to be sure, the revolution has a long way to go before the former monarch—secularization theory—will be fully overthrown. Catherine Brekus's new volume *The Religious History of American Women*, for example, begins with a bracingly critical essay pointing out how inadequately American religious historians have incorporated women into their stories in a way that fundamentally alters the very questions we ask about the past, as opposed to the "add women and stir" method, which leaves the prevailing assumptions as they are and simply adds a token paragraph about women actually existing.[2]

That being said, it bears repeating that the guild of history has been in the business of "getting" religion, and scholars from church-related schools have had a lot to do with that. I would even argue, against the position of many of my colleagues who feel more beleaguered or embattled, that the historical guild is a relatively amenable place for scholars of faith, as well as for scholars who study faith. Those who do military history or economic history, I might suggest, probably have a greater reason to feel slighted. Their fields have been out of fashion (not in the worlds of public history or popular history, where military history is all too popular, but specifically within groups such as the American Historical Association) and more neglected than is the case with religious history. Recently, in fact, a few historians in public debates have actually complained that religion has been getting too much attention in recent discussions of American history. They may or may not be right, but the fact that such an assertion can be plausibly made shows how far we have come, as well, perhaps, as the certain sense of resentment that it has engendered.

One remaining battle in the guild centers on distinguishing between religion in America and the Religious Right. Secularist friends and critics love to conflate the two, as a means, in part, of keeping their distance even from religious sentiment and activism of the past—such as the antislavery movement—which they like. I was reminded of this recently in reading a review of an outstanding recent book in American religious, historical, and literary studies: Joanna Brooks's *American Lazarus: Religion and the Rise of Native American and African American Literature*.[4] At the end of a mostly positive overview of this work, which traces the influence of Protestant evangelicalism on the birth and rise of the very earliest pieces of Native and African American literature in American history, the reviewer said, in effect, that she just didn't feel like giving religion such positive credit, that it left her feeling grumpy, and then went on to list the usual suspects of bad religious figures and movements, ranging from the Religious Right to George W. Bush. Works such as those of Joanna Brooks, the reviewer concluded, inadvertently might help the cause of religion—and by "religion," the reviewer meant right-wing stuff that she didn't like.[5]

To be sure, the history of conservatism in America is much in vogue now, for the very good reason that we don't know very much about it, and this history contains a healthy dollop of religion. Darren Dochuk has written beautifully on the subject, while the historian Kevin Kruse of Princeton is currently examining the Sunbelt origins of the religious right, and George Marsden's studies of fundamentalism have been carried forward into new eras and gendered analyses of the meaning of conservative women's movements (including Marie Griffith's memorable study of the Women Aglow phenomenon and the meaning of the rhetoric of "submission" among conservative women).[6] There is no doubt that, for many historians, "religion" and "right" are two terms which no man can put asunder, never mind that, aside from the musings of pious slaveholders, the confluence of democratic evangelicalism and political conservatism is a very recent development indeed.

Secularist colleagues—including my own colleague in medieval history, who has written profoundly and beautifully of a fourteenth-century German cult involving a young peasant boy who claimed to see visions of angels ordering him to kill priests—would likely have a difficult time with my many, many students who arrive at class after their day's work at Focus on the Family; or who attend one of our numerous megachurches; or who will not watch the Civil War movie *Glory* or read Ralph Ellison's *Invisible Man* because it somehow offends their religious preconceptions; or who, when honest and not just spouting back what they think I want to hear, will provide spiritual and teleologically charged explanations for events that historians explain through secular frameworks; or who engage in over-heated classroom polemics about whether Joseph Smith or James Dobson are prophets or charlatans. They would find comfort, however, in my students who come to class speaking of their last Wiccan meeting; or of the village atheists who delight in "pimping" the self-acknowledged religious students; or, of course, of the considerable body of students whose religious philosophy can best be summed up as "yeah, whatever."

When I tell history colleagues elsewhere that I teach in Colorado Springs, their first reaction is usually that I must ski all the time—not true! Their second (and sometimes their first) reaction is, "Well, isn't that place a little bit, you know, wacky," and I know they are thinking of our reputation as a center for religious activism, mostly associated with the Right. Focus on the Family is the best-known of the lot, but certainly there are dozens of others, and many of my students come from those groups. My colleagues' response is an attempt to be sympathetic with me—how beleaguered and oppressed I must feel, they seem to imply, surrounded by fundamentalist fanatics. In fact, though, there could scarcely be a better place for someone who seeks students genuinely interested in engaging with America's religious past, and who know in their own souls why it must be taken seriously and studied respectfully. I don't have to deal with the "so what" question. And honestly, I don't feel that I've had to deal, at least very much, with that in the larger guild. So I feel fortunate that a social history revolution designed for very different purposes has, however accidentally, given religion a place at the intellectual table of American history; and that I have such ongoing and vital contact with students who do not dismiss religion (as might be common in other state schools), or who take it for granted as the common language of their culture, as was, I think, the case at my own church-related college, Oklahoma Baptist University, where I got my BA. Instead, my teaching situation allows me to think fruitfully and nearly daily about the relationship of religion to the public square, and to hash out all the complicated questions that come out of that.

Where I think the true danger lies is in the larger sense of the disconnection of academia from public life and purpose. Academia bears its share of fault for this, and that share of fault seems to be scrutinized and agonized about constantly, not least by historians who are always wondering why no one reads their book unless it happens to be about a Founding Father, a Great Civil War Battle, or a Famous Sexual Scandal from the past (I'm exaggerating, of course, but not by all that much). I've had some experience with this side of things in Colorado, too, and I would like to conclude with that story. In my years here, I guess, I have become religiously committed to the survival and further development of public higher education, partially because of the relentless series of attacks it undergoes, and partially because our peculiarly distorted taxation and fiscal budgeting policies in the state of Colorado mean that higher education always and by default takes the largest "hit" in a time of a state budget downturn—most recently, to the tune of a nearly 40 percent overall state budget cut in the years 2002–2005.

A few years ago, the gadfly David Horowitz came through town, looking for a few professors to egg on in debate. Foolishly, I took him up on it, forgetting a basic historical principle—that debate with a fundamentally dishonest polemicist is always stupid—and forgetting also that I would immediately be classed with the likes of Ward Churchill, who was at that time instantly famous for his egregiously and inexcusably stupid, albeit free-speech protected, comments about 9/11 victims. Not to bore with details, but an exchange posted on the Internet led to a response by a radio polemicist named Mike Rosen, host of the largest AM talk radio show in the state of Colorado, in the form of a newspaper editorial. This produced from me a brief letter published in response, which then produced an entire, hour-long episode of Rosen's show devoted to ME! I didn't hear it and didn't even know it was on, as I happened to be teaching that hour (one of Rosen's contentions, I should add, was that professors at Colorado's public universities never taught, since they hated students and teaching, in addition, of course, to hating America, and forced their graduate students to do all their teaching for them). However, somebody later sent me a tape of the episode, where I heard Rosen say things such as "perhaps someone could call in and report on [add sinister voice here] *Professor Harvey's ideological inclinations.*" Following the program, and before I had heard it or even knew that such a thing had transpired, I was deluged with hate email from all over the state. Apparently, they objected to highly controversial statements I had made, such as that historians do their best to weigh the evidence carefully and present as rich and nuanced a view of historical events as they can in the classroom and not to "politicize" issues. Naturally, the listeners took this to mean that I, like all professors, politicized subjects to favor "the Left," and denounced or at least graded unfairly those who took up views from "the Right."

This incident blew over quickly, as Ward Churchill proved a far juicier target than a justly obscure history professor such as myself. Nonetheless, it made me think of the basic values of historians, and what we bring into our research and our teaching. It also made me think hard about a comment a number of students have made in recent years during various religious history classes that I have taught—that they could not tell what I "believed in," so they had to ask. My consistent response has been to refuse to answer, telling them that my job is to help them explore religious beliefs in a historical context, and that these issues are sensitive and divisive enough, especially in our very politicized town, that I feel it best, in the context of a state-supported university, to keep my convictions to myself for the purpose of these classes. My immediate colleagues surrounding me—a devout atheist who teaches medieval history and the history of Christianity on the one side, and a devout Episcopalian who teaches German and Jewish history on the other side—take very different stances, making their own convictions clear upfront at the beginning of the semester. I don't claim that one stance is better than another. Indeed, I value the diversity and variety just in the first three doors of my hallway. We have very different religious convictions; we think about and teach history very differently; and we learn from each other and relish each other's intellectual company. Most important here, I think, is the feeling that Christian scholars (or atheist scholars, for that matter, or whoever) who take up oppositional stances against their guilds risk losing some very important protections and freedoms which those guilds provide them. Moreover, while the guilds promote scholarly objectivity and neutrality, those values depend on deeper moralities of fairness, justice, and (for the historian) empathy. The Mike Rosen episode recounted above was more amusing than frightening to me, in part because I knew my state-supported university and my historical associations had supported and valued my forays into research and teaching in American religious history.

I don't know yet how best to communicate how I value this to a larger public. My sense is that the larger public, at least in my state, believes that scholars who aren't in the sciences, and maybe even those who are, produce what amounts to propaganda which has no more value in the larger marketplace of ideas than any other ranting blogger or bloviating talking head. This is why, I think, our students have such difficulty distinguishing between "opinion" and "argument." Haven't we all heard it—"You just mean you want my opinion, right," after I have just told them "I'm looking for you to make a solid argument based on a clear thesis supported by concrete evidence drawn from your research." The culture of opinion threatens to render irrelevant the pursuit of scholarly excellence, and this is a trend which I hope our scholarly guilds will resist with firm religious conviction.

Endnotes

1. Paul Harvey, *Freedom's Coming: Religious Culture and the Shaping of the South from the Civil War through the Civil Rights Era* (Chapel Hill, NC: University of North Carolina Press, 2005).

2. Catherine Brekus, ed., *The Religious History of American Women: Reimagining the Past* (Chapel Hill, NC: University of North Carolina Press, 2007).

3. David A. Hollinger, "Enough Already: Universities Do Not Need More Christianity," in *Religion, Scholarship, & Higher Education: Perspectives, Models, and Future Prospects*, ed. Andrea Sterk, pp. 40–49 (Notre Dame, IN: University of Notre Dame Press, 2002).

4. Joanna Brooks, *American Lazarus: Religion and the Rise of African-American and Native American Literatures* (New York: Oxford University, 2003).

5. Laura Murray, review of *American Lazarus* by Joanna Brooks, *Early American Literature* Vol. 40 No. 2 (June 2005): pp. 395–402.

6. Darren Dochuk, *From Bible Belt to Sunbelt: Plain-Folk Religion, Grassroots Politics, and the Rise of Evangelical Conservatism* (New York: W. W. Norton, forthcoming 2010); George Marsden, *Fundamentalism and American Culture: The Shaping of Twentieth-Century Evangelicalism 1870–1925*, (New York: Oxford University, 1980); R. Marie Griffith, *God's Daughters: Evangelical Women and the Power of Submission* (Berkeley, CA: University of California Press, 2000).

CHAPTER FIVE

My Teaching Load Is None of Your Business, and Don't Steal My Desk

Seeking an Identity among Academic Guilds

Maria LaMonaca

Although a Lilly Postdoctoral Fellowship is only two years in duration (in my case, from 1999 to 2001), there are some sharp distinctions drawn between first and second-year postdoctoral fellows. As a first-year fellow, I shared a thinly-partitioned basement office with Mike Utzinger and Kathleen Cummings, where we conducted long and often hilarious conversations through the walls, at the expense, no doubt, of our teaching and research. We knew we were second-year fellows and truly grown up, however, when we were allowed to move into the relatively posh, fantastically huge offices on the first floor of Linwood House. I still remember the great window view I had of a beautiful old tree and the Chapel of the Resurrection beyond.

I used to think that my Lilly Postdoc was my first "real world" job, until I realized, at my first tenure-track job, how privileged and sheltered I had been in so many ways. For example, I noticed that, while some of my new colleagues at Columbia College could see trees from their office windows, none of them had views of the largest collegiate chapel in the United States. Shocking! Even more disconcerting, I had neither a tree nor a chapel view, as Columbia's English department was (and still is) located in the basement of the college library. But I decided to make the best of things. I decorated my walls with the classiest-looking framed prints I could find, and one day, about a month before classes started, I descended to my office and found a wonderful surprise: the facilities plant had sent over a highly polished, real wood executive desk. I felt like a grownup again!

My bliss was short-lived, however. My office neighbors informed me that my then-department chair had plans to transfer my desk to her office, since she had, in her words, "worked here for thirty years and never had a new desk." I was crushed. At that early stage in my career, I needed nice furniture and all the trappings to feel like a professional. I went to my chair and pleaded for my desk. My chair—who is, in fact, a wonderful person and by now a close friend—understood. I got to keep my new desk, although it helped that another person in my department was willing to sacrifice hers.

Why this long story about a desk? The desk incident symbolizes for me a breaking point, between my sheltered preparation for academia and the moment I found myself immersed in the real-world dynamics of it, with all the accompanying struggles for both professional recognition and limited material resources. On a larger level, the desk represents for me all the things one takes for granted in academia. You may sit down to work at your desk every day, but when was the last time you thought about the desk itself? How many drawers does it have? What do the pulls or knobs look like? Where are the ink stains and the rings from your coffee mug? The desk is the seldom-examined, literal foundation for one's work, and in that sense, it can also be a metaphor for the professional guild: those standards, attitudes, and assumptions undergirding our academic work, often without our conscious awareness of them.

Every time I try to define for myself my "academic guild," however, I feel a kind of disorientation, similar to what I might feel if I didn't know where my own desk was located. This has everything to do with my overlapping yet distinctive professional roles: both a faculty member at a small, teaching-intensive, Methodist-affiliated college, and a scholar who works hard to remain an active member of an international academic community. In my day-to-day life on the campus of Columbia College, I feel myself part of one academic guild, but at my research conferences and in interactions with colleagues in my scholarly field, I am very much part of another. As a Christian scholar, I do not favor one over the other, because I have found, in both realms, experiences that gratify and reinforce my most cherished personal values.

In the guild of my larger scholarly community, I have found enormous support, mentoring, and encouragement for the book I have finally finished, after nearly ten years of research and writing. The book is about Catholicism and Victorian culture, but in a larger sense, it is also about Victorian Protestantism and the conflicting discourses of Christianity and secularism in the modern world. The project holds deeply personal, as well as professional, significance for me. The critical approaches I employ stem directly from the understanding of religious belief I have acquired in my thirty-five years as a practicing Roman Catholic.

My religious identity has provided me with a unique perspective on my topic, and so far, my academic guild has proven to be a receptive audience. Over ten years ago, Jenny Franchot labeled religion as an "invisible domain" in the secular field of literary studies—an overlooked topic that no serious scholar was willing to touch. Franchot's assessment of the academy was a valid one, but by the time her article appeared in 1995, things were already changing.[1] Since the mid-1990s, my field has witnessed a small explosion of books on religious topics. The current fascination with both identity politics and cultural studies has encouraged scholars to view religion's influence on individuals and cultures in more sophisticated, multifaceted ways. This sea change has been very fortunate for me and my book, in that I have found interest for my work beyond circles devoted to Christianity and literature. I regularly present excerpts from the book at secular conferences, the book's funding includes grants from the National Endowment for the Humanities, and it will be published by Ohio State University Press. I do not know whether the book itself will do well, but the process of writing it may be reward enough for me. It was a spiritual, as well as intellectual, workout, and I thank God for granting me the patience, focus, and determination to see this project through, after so many years.

W hile my scholarly guild provides one kind of validation for me as a Christian academic, my environment at Columbia College provides another. My guild at Columbia College is definitely a teaching-oriented one, and I see my work in the classroom as another type of spiritual exercise. Teaching challenges me in all the areas where I need the most work. An introvert by nature, I become an extravert to lead class. Constitutionally impatient, I learn patience as I work with students. A bookworm who sees texts as the fount of all knowledge, I am constantly humbled and delighted by students made wise by life experience, not an exhaustive reading of Shakespeare.

Columbia College's unique environment provides further rewards for me as a teacher. I work with a small student body—all women in the day program, and a coed working adult population in the evening program. A large percentage of our students are first-generation college students. Nearly one-third are African American. I work with students who see education as a privilege, not an entitlement. Once in a while, I get the sense that, through teaching them, I might be making a difference. Along with excellent teaching, my college guild also privileges service to others. This value is evident not just in warm, supportive relationships between teachers and students, but also in relationships among faculty and staff. The campus community provides an enormous level of support when one of its own suffers an illness, a bereavement, or some other life crisis. My own department feels like an extended family.

Although I have found a niche, as a Christian academic, in each of my guilds, this fact also makes me keenly aware of conflicts and contradictions between the two. These conflicts, of course, reflect ongoing tensions in higher education as a whole. I feel the most disorientation about guild allegiances and scholarly identity when I attend professional conferences. I love attending conferences, but I have found, coming from a small college with a regional student body, that I am constantly fielding questions about my job satisfaction. The most common questions I get are, "Do you like it there?" "What's your teaching load?" Usually, I reply that yes, I like it there, and that my teaching load is four courses per semester. At this point, the questioner usually adopts a pitying expression, as if I just revealed that I had a wasting terminal ill-ness. "You're kidding," my questioner replies, "how on earth do you survive?" My favorite response, however, came from a gradu-ate student I ran into a few years ago. Although yet to go on the job market himself, he blurted out, "If I had to teach four courses a semester, I'd hang myself!"

Now, I will admit that four courses a semester is a formidable load. This issue is being discussed on our campus, and I am optimis-tic that the college will move to lighter loads in the near future. My point is that the reactions I get to my teaching load seem wildly disproportionate to what the situation actually warrants. I may feel overworked sometimes, but I am neither in a state of desperation, nor ready to commit suicide. With good organization and discipline, I still find time to eat, sleep, exercise regularly, and continue my research agenda. I still have far more leisure time throughout the year than my husband, who works in the corporate sector. I am left with the conviction that the exaggerated responses to my teaching load have more to do with the academy's ambivalent attitude toward teaching than with my individual situation. At these same confer-ences, I overhear people with 3/2 loads and 2/2 loads complain about how time-consuming teaching is, and what little time they have for scholarship.

The guild I encounter at my research conferences sustains me as a scholar, but it has little to say to me regarding my teaching, other than that it is rather burdensome and I should do less of it. Yet as a Christian academic, I cannot underestimate the importance of teaching. I must do meaningful work that makes a contribution to society. In the classroom, I see this happening. I don't see dra-matic results every day, but I cannot doubt, when I stand before my students, the nature of the work that God has called me to do. The differences I can or will make through scholarship seem far more abstract and tenuous. Of course, we all dream that our scholarship will change peoples' lives or radically alter standard assumptions in our respective fields of study. But in this era of rising expectations for scholarly publishing, my new book, when it hits the shelves, will compete for attention among hundreds, even thousands, of other new scholarly titles. Who has time to read them all?

Decades ago, publishing even one book was a significant lifetime achievement: one could head off to retirement in a rosy glow of triumph. Today, things are different. My book manuscript is still in the copy editing stages, yet people are already asking me what book number two will be about. Not only do these expectations diminish the book I have managed to write, but they also raise some serious questions for me, given my research interests. I already have described how receptive my field has become to religious topics. Yet this tolerance, as I am discovering, has its limits. The same scholars who were enthusiastic readers of my first book manuscript are now warning me *not* to write a second book on religion. "You might get pigeonholed," they say. I find this concern perplexing, because I know that no one would bat an eye if I wrote three books on Victorian economics or six on Victorian science. One literary study on religion reveals a scholar's professional interest in the topic, it seems, but two studies hint at personal beliefs best kept under wraps. As I reflect upon future directions for my research, I remind myself that, whatever I do write on in the future, it must be something I consider vital and relevant to both myself and others. Like many scholars of Victorian literature, I suspect, I remain haunted by George Eliot's characterization of Edward Casaubon in *Middlemarch*, laboring for years on his completely useless *Key to All Mythologies*.

Eliot's ineffectual scholar, Casaubon, warns us that the ignorance or denial of real life warps both individuals and communities. As much as I enjoy my larger scholarly guild, I believe it can take a few lessons from the guild of the small, teaching-intensive college. Our work must matter in the world, and teaching always reminds me of this. My work in the classroom makes me feel like a "real bunny," not just a velveteen rabbit. Reciprocally, the teaching guild can take something valuable from the scholarship guild. I am not proposing that faculty at small, teaching-intensive colleges suddenly be expected to churn out a lot of scholarship. A small, but significant, percentage of the Columbia College faculty does engage in regular, serious scholarship, well beyond requirements for tenure and promotion. Although all schools of higher education have an obligation, I believe, to support faculty scholarship as resources permit, schools like Columbia also provide a home for those many excellent teachers who feel little or no call toward a life of research.

But what all campus communities need—whether they are large research institutions or small colleges—is an affirmation of the value and significance of faculty time. At research universities, it is acceptable to demand time for one's scholarship. At teaching-intensive colleges, how does one frame a request for time? At campuses where service to others is paramount, requests for time, even to engage in scholarship, can appear suspiciously self-indulgent. And the Christian faculty member, who also sees her work in terms of service, risks internalizing the belief that *all* her time and energy must go directly toward supporting students and the campus community. But as George Eliot's fictional heroines learn in one novel after another, service to others and a rejection of egoism are not achieved through self-sacrifice. Healthy individuals strike a balance between charity toward others and charity toward self. All faculty engaged in the business of teaching and learning need time, if not for scholarship, then for other kinds of development, both professional and personal. And at church-related institutions, shouldn't there also be time for prayer, spiritual renewal, and meditation?

The academy is counter-cultural in many ways, including its work schedules. There are few professions besides education that permit full-time workers entire weeks and months off for Christmas, fall and spring breaks, and summer recess. Of course, faculty members do continue to work during these periods, planning classes, doing research, and sometimes, they continue teaching. But in this system, there is recognition that individuals can be trusted to use their time well. It is not a corporate idea of time, where every hour, documented and billable, must result in a concrete product. For this reason, even in a teaching-intensive environment, I have far more leisure time than my husband. As we contemplate starting a family, however, I realize that my hours of free time are probably numbered. And I am not so naïve to assume that my friends and colleagues at research institutions—many of whom are also excellent teachers, by the way— spend their days sipping sherry and pondering life's great questions. Although it is acceptable in the culture of the research university to actively seek time for scholarship, faculty schedules can still be very hectic. If this is not because of teaching loads per se, it is due to huge classes, committee work, faculty searches, and other duties involved in running a university.

I only hope that, as colleges and universities increasingly resemble corporations at the administrative levels, we remember that the appreciation of unstructured time—time not filled with television, Internet, or text messaging, I might add—is as important a life lesson for our students as an appreciation for literature or the ability to think critically. How do we prepare students, especially as Christian academics, for working in America, a country in which people clock more hours on the job than most other industrialized nations? How do we model balanced lives? Not, I suspect, with dark circles under our eyes by midterm. As Christian academics, we must be mindful that we are shaping the "whole person," not just another drone in the American workforce. And if we are concerned about our students' spiritual health, then we must somehow teach the value of reflection, contemplation, and free time. This has implications for our students' well-being, and also for the larger good of society. In his journals, Buddhist monk and writer Thich Nhat Hanh discusses the danger of what he calls "the premature hero":

> Life waits patiently for true heroes. It is dangerous when those aspiring to be heroes cannot wait until they find themselves. When aspiring heroes have not found themselves, they are tempted to borrow the world's weapons—money, fame, and power—to fight their battles. These weapons cannot protect the inner life of the hero. To cope with his fears and insecurities, the premature hero has to stay busy all the time. The destructive capacity of nonstop busyness rivals nuclear weapons and is as addictive as opium. It empties the life of the spirit.[2]

In this passage, Hanh pinpoints constant busyness as a formidable obstacle to the life of the spirit; it keeps individuals from finding themselves and, by association, their rightful work in the world. As I chart my growth as a teacher and a scholar between two distinct, and at times contradictory, academic guilds, I find it intriguing that I end up making a loud call for more free time. I have learned, from my teaching-intensive guild, that a life of scholarship—at least for me—must be grounded in the solid, time-consuming realities of the classroom. But I have learned from my research guild that I can say "no" to nonstop service sometimes, whether to write my next article, or more importantly, to regain my sanity and equilibrium.

In the end, perhaps my loud calls for time and balance say as much, if not more, about me than about the state of the academy. When I was a postdoctoral fellow, I participated earnestly in discussions about the formation of the "whole person," and we also read Dorothy Bass's fine book, *Receiving the Day: Christian Practices for Opening the Gift of Time*.[3] Bass's portrayal of time as a sacred gift to be cherished, not squandered, resonated with me six years ago, but I understand her points, and the notion of the "whole person," in a far deeper way now. I was a certifiable workaholic in graduate school, and I pushed myself hard as a postdoc as well. And although I may spend just as many hours, if not more, working at my tenure track-job, my priorities and values have definitely shifted. I cannot take my positive teaching evaluations, my articles, or my book to the grave. My talents are a gift from God, but so is my time, and I need to value and enjoy it to the fullest. How can I teach this to my students? I might not have as much free time as I'd like, but I can at least stop looking so frantically busy. Perhaps the first step is to clean off the top of my desk.

Endnotes

1. Jenny Franchot, "Invisible Domain: Religion and American Literary Studies," *American Literature* Vol. 67 (December 1995): pp. 833–842.

2. Robert Ellsberg, ed., *Thich Nhat Hanh: Essential Writings* (Maryknoll, NY: Orbis Books, 2001), p. 44.

3. Dorothy C. Bass, *Receiving the Day: Christian Practices for Opening the Gift of Time* (San Francisco: Jossey-Bass, 2001).

CHAPTER SIX

The Profession Is The World

Some Thoughts on Being in the Guild But Not of It

Heath White

My thesis is simple. It is that what we call the academic profession, or guild, is one aspect or sphere of what the Bible calls "the world." As Christians, we believe that the kingdom of God has begun breaking into the world, and that this process will continue in some form until our Lord returns. The academic profession is not immune from this breaking-in process, nor from all that goes with it. That is how we ought to think about our guilds.

Two concepts require clarification before it can really be clear what I'm talking about: "the guild" and "the world."

What does it mean to be in a professional guild? How am I, a professional philosopher employed at a university, for example, different from someone who simply studies philosophy on the side, or from someone with a PhD who has left the profession? Here are a few of the rights, privileges, and responsibilities of guild membership:

* Guild members typically teach in a university setting. They are the front-line representatives of their discipline in educational institutions.

* Guild members do original research, presenting papers and publishing articles and books, which

51

advance and expand (or allege to advance and expand) the knowledge and insight that the discipline has to offer.

* Guild members have a credential, and a social position, that enables them to speak with some (albeit limited) authority on the topics of their expertise, and sometimes, outside those topics.

* Guild members often enjoy tenure, which allows them to speak very freely to their students and the public.

* Guild members do the legwork that maintains the guild system: They run their departments and much of the university, they do the peer review that sustains published research at a professional level, and they maintain the professional organizations of their guild.

In short—and I am not being particularly original here—an academic guild is a self-perpetuating community devoted to the three traditional areas of teaching, research, and service.

Now for the more difficult and interesting question: What is "the world," Biblically conceived? I had to confront this issue seriously, for the first time, when I taught the Gospels in Valparaiso University's Christ College Freshman Seminar. The best analogy I could discover was that, in the eyes of the gospel writers, "the world" is what we might call "occupied territory."

Imagine yourself as a French citizen back in, say, 1943. The Nazis have rolled over your country and are running the joint. You have been contacted by the resistance. They have some Good News for you. The Allies are coming! Although France is at present an enemy of the Allies, the Allies have nevertheless loved your France enough to send their own sons to die in order to liberate her. The size of the Allied force means that the outcome of the battle is a foregone conclusion; it's just a matter of time, though there is plenty of action ahead.

As a partisan, your job, in the interim, is to do what you can to advance the rule and reign of freedom in your country. No one expects you to overthrow the Nazis yourself, and even the whole resistance movement will not be sufficient for victory. The Allies can do the job without you, but you can help, too, and your efforts can make life a little more hopeful and bearable for many people while you wait. Your participation in the resistance is both a way of assisting the good guys, who will ultimately be victorious, and also a way of placing yourself on that side. Your battle is not, properly speaking, against other French folk, your own flesh and blood, but against the Nazi principalities and powers which rule your country in its present dark time.

Though the regime is oppressive, much of life still goes on as before. There are still crops to raise, factories to run—and classes to teach. People still celebrate birthdays and anniversaries, weddings and deaths—and graduations. Some aspects of life are touched more by the new regime than others—certain business incentives are altered; the state is more intrusive; there is more cronyism and corruption. Some parts of the university are left alone; some continue much as before, but are encouraged or required to teach regime-friendly doctrine; a few parts of the university are simply propaganda organs. The degree to which individuals have been co-opted, and institutions pressured or corrupted, varies tremendously.

Though everyone would be better off, objectively speaking, if France were liberated, of any given French person, it is impossible to say whether they will welcome news of the invasion. If you tell people that the Allies are coming, some will think you are hopelessly naïve. Some collaborators may persecute you. Others, fearing to cross the Nazi regime, will declare their sympathies in private, but do nothing risky. Yet others are willing to do the right thing even without the encouragement of the good news. A few, who have both hope and courage, will join the resistance with you.

This parable, like all parables, is imperfect, but I think it is instructive. "The world" is not simply the physical planet, or the collection of people on it. It is the system of political and social—and professional—relations in which those people live. From one angle, this system remains, in the university as elsewhere, basically normal, retaining the imprint of its initial good creation. In this sense, Christians can gladly participate in the world alongside non-believers, in fundamental cooperation. From another angle, in that it is a fallen world, we can expect it to contain elements of opposition to things of God, and where these elements crop up, Christians must oppose the world and expect conflict when doing so. From a third angle, in that God loves his creation and especially the people in it, he intends to redeem the world, and Christians have the obligation to assist in this healing process, which is liable to attract some cooperation, some conflict, and a fair bit of apathy. We Christian academics, exercising discernment to separate cases, have to take up all three attitudes toward our profession, as part of living in the world but not of it: glad participation in a good created order, firm opposition to distortions in the profession introduced by the fall, and redemptive activity that restores the profession to wholeness, in both articulated theory and lived example.

Obviously, I know most about my own situation, as a philosopher in a mid-level state university, so I will start there. Philosophy, etymologically, is the love of wisdom. Slightly less poetically, philosophy is all about asking "big questions": thinking about human nature, God, society, justice, and the good life, all in the clearest, most rationally penetrating way we can. Of course, if you ever pick up a philosophy journal, you will realize that asking the big questions devolves very quickly, at the professional level, into asking the teensy-weensy questions. But I've heard that other disciplines have the same problem.

I think this formal goal of philosophy—asking big questions, pursuing wisdom and understanding—is a beautiful thing, a corollary of our creation as free, rational creatures in the image of God. Human beings always have and always will ask these kinds of questions, and as a teacher of philosophy, I have the privilege of introducing my students, Christian and non-Christian, into this aspect of their humanity and helping them deepen it. I have secular colleagues who have much the same view of their vocation, though without the religious background. And though we do not share a theological footing, my colleagues and I can appreciate each others' contributions to the development of our students.

There are ways in which this pursuit of wisdom can become corrupted, however. There is, of course, the student who views the assignments as hoops to be jumped through and consequently wants to know which positions in her papers will be most pleasing to the teacher. There is the student who delights in virtuoso argumentation and displays his command of the literature, an undertaking done for its own sake, rather than for the sake of finding the truth. These students are not polishing their divine image; they are intent on polishing their resumes. How to bring such students to care about the topic, rather than care about looking good on paper? Sometimes, I can throw them back on their own devices. When they come up to me after class, wanting to know which paper topic they should write on, I ask, "Which topic interests you the most?" Sometimes, I can just teach a little harder, and show from its impact on (as it's called) "real life" why free will is worth thinking about. Sometimes, I can teach this by example. And sometimes, I can do nothing—such students are often confirmed in their careerism by the time they get to me.

Here is probably my sharpest challenge. Many of my students are convinced, even after several weeks of philosophy with me, that philosophical questions have no answers. Think about that. If it is true, what's the point of doing philosophy? (Which is why I desperately hope it isn't true!) But it's not just the relevance of my discipline that is at stake here; and the theme of hope is no accident. For this widespread attitude of, "it's all just a matter of opinion" and "whatever you think, that's true for you" is really a form of despair: an absence of hope that there is any truth to be known about God, or who we are, or what we can be confident of, or what is worth pursuing in life. And gripped by this despair, which on most days is more enervating than anguishing, they allow the course of their lives to be set by their vague inclinations, or their parents, or the lures and pressures of the wider culture, without making the effort to think through their position in the wider world. They do not make this effort, because, in their despair, it seems futile.[1]

How to help such students? I struggle and struggle with this question. I have slick arguments which show that such positions are self-refuting and cannot be consistently held. But statements like "It's all relative" express, as I said, a lack of hope; they are not so much a metaphysic or an epistemology as they are an ethic. What I desire to do is give my students a sense of hope, a sense that intellectual effort, pursued with integrity, can pay off. And I have found no other way of doing this, really, than to model it. I just go into class, day after day, treating philosophical questions as if they matter, and philosophical theories as if they might be answers. Sometimes, eventually, this rubs off.

At the professional, research level, there is a different kind of challenge to being in the guild but not of it. Philosophy, as I said, is, at its core, the love of wisdom, the search for understanding about deep questions, but there are at least two ways this can go wrong in the contemporary academy.

For one thing, it is very easy to become a micro-specialist and lose sight of any questions that people would fundamentally care about. Moreover, this incipient superficiality is rewarded by the discipline in the form of judging an academic's publications by their quantity, rather than by their quality, and by rewarding research efforts over teaching efforts. A Christian needs to keep his eye on the ball.

There is a second way in which the research imperative can go awry. Every discipline is a part of God's good creation. I already stated the way I see philosophy fitting into this, but it is also not infrequently true that disciplines become captive to particular theories or movements that acquire the status of disciplinary dogma. Failure to subscribe to the dogma renders you a marginal member of the discipline at some level. The fairly recent history of Anglo-American philosophy illustrates this tendency very well. At one point in philosophy, the dogma was an extreme empiricism: only experience yielded knowledge, only what could be experienced was real, and the only meaningful language was what could be cashed out in terms of experience. Thankfully, philosophy is past that era. But there is another dogma in philosophy at present, *naturalism*: the view that the natural is all there is, or roughly, that reality is fully described by some eschatological version of the sciences. You can tell that naturalism is a disciplinary dogma in philosophy, because it is virtually the only position which analytic philosophers are eager to sign on to, but not eager to define precisely. (Usually, it's the other way around.) Naturalism is not a view narrowly confined to philosophy: Its picture of human beings as one more item in a world of causes, but no reasons, provides the background for Nietzsche's moral nihilism and Foucault's social determinism, views which are widely influential in the humanities and social sciences. There are some reasons to believe naturalism, just as there were some reasons to believe the hard-core empiricism that gave it birth. But ultimately, they are expressions of an anti-theistic worldview, and in the last analysis, these views are emissaries of hell.

Christian philosophers have a success story to tell about the first phase, of anti-theistic empiricism. Christian philosophers played a significant, though by no means exclusive, role in killing it off, using philosophical arguments, the tools of the discipline. One moral of this story is that the antidote to bad philosophy is better philosophy, but that is not the only moral. What made the difference among the Christian philosophers at work was, first, a confidence that all truth is God's truth, so there *must* be good arguments against hard-core empiricism; and second, a willingness to stick to one's guns, literally for decades, in the face of serious disciplinary pressure.

So far, there is no similar success story to be told regarding the influence of naturalism. Some attempts to refute it have been made, and Christian thinkers are not the only ones interested in making such attempts. But naturalism remains, for the present, very influential and very unfriendly to Christian thought. The remedy will be patience, confidence, perseverance—and better philosophy. I imagine that many teachers in the humanities can identify similar challenges in their own disciplines.

I have been exploring the idea that our guilds are one sphere of the world, and as Christians, that is how we must relate to them. There is a past, a present, and a future involved here. As to the past, we need to keep in mind that God was in Christ reconciling the world—even, I venture, our academic professional world—to himself. He created it; he loved it; so must we love it, too. For the future, we are promised that, one day, the knee of every philosopher,

historian, theologian, literature professor, musicologist, and drama-
tist will bow, and all their tongues confess that Jesus is Lord; and I
don't think they will cease to be philosophers, historians, and so on
on that day. And for our present, both as an encouraging promise
and a humbling challenge, we have Christ's words: "You are the
light of the world."

Endnotes

1. I first ran across this diagnosis of relativism as despair in "An Ignatian
Approach to Teaching Philosophy" by Elizabeth Murray Morelli, in *Teaching as
an Act of Faith*, ed. Arlin C. Migliazzo (New York: Fordham University Press,
2004). I was struck at the time by the insight of the diagnosis, and my respect
for its wisdom has only deepened with time.

CHAPTER SEVEN

Faith That Kills?

Reflections on Religion after 9/11

J. Michael Utzinger

When I was a younger scholar searching for an academic position, I was asked by an historian during an interview reception whether I was a Christian.

Puzzled, I answered, "Yes."

"Then, would you kill in the name of Christ?"

Now shocked (but admittedly quite bemused and intrigued), I responded, "No."

The historian smiled, having sprung his "trap," and asked, "Then how can you say that you are serious about your faith, if you are not willing to do the most difficult thing you can be asked to do?" At this point, other faculty members noticed that this individual was alone with me and moved to whisk me away.

I later spoke with this individual again. I might summarize his argument as follows: "If you really believe that your faith is absolutely true, then you are duty bound to spread that message at any cost (even violence). Tolerance is an abrogation of one's religious duty (and love of neighbor, since you are essentially helping consign those you tolerate to hell)—tolerant Christians, therefore, are not serious Christians." My response came naturally, "I am serious because I actually listen to what Jesus said." After all, it is hard to imagine how one can genuinely justify violent behavior in the name of a faith that promotes such maxims as "blessed are the peacemakers" or "do not repay evil with evil." He remained unconvinced.

What draws me to this story is not its shock value. Rather, I am interested in why he was unconvinced by my response. He was not calling religious folk hypocrites for not practicing what they preach. Rather, the premise behind his rejection was the assumption that violent religious extremism is the face of vital expressions of religion in the modern world. This conflation of religious violence with religious vitality, I would argue, did not allow him to take religion (mine or anyone else's) as a genuine human phenomenon. I am further drawn to this anecdote because I do not think that this individual's argument is an anomaly in our current cultural climate or the academy. And this worries me. I am worried that religion's newfound popularity is premised on ideas that ultimately undermine our ability to take religion and religious people seriously.

If religion is alive and well in the current American consciousness, it is not hard to see why. Since the late-1970s, government officials, businesspersons, journalists, and academics have had no choice but to notice conservative, often reactionary, forms of "fundamentalism" rising as a phoenix from the ashes of religion's quite exaggerated death. The formation of the Islamic Republic in Iran, calls of *jihad* against the Soviet Union in Afghanistan, mass suicide at Jonestown in Guyana, and the formation of the Moral Majority in the United States were but a few examples of renewed religious activity in the world at that time. Fast-forward to September 12, 2001, the day after the terrorist attacks in New York and Washington; suddenly, the vitality of religion in the modern world seemed terrifyingly obvious to all Americans.

In fact, since 9/11, a new popular truism has replaced the idea that religion was a passing stage in human history. Religion has now morphed into something reactive, militant, and violent. More to the point, it has become something too dangerous to ignore. For the year 2006, the top two stories about religion, as ranked by American journalists, concerned religion and violence. The top story of the year was the worldwide violent Muslim reaction to the cartoons

of Muhammad published in Denmark. The second was Pope Benedict XVI's indelicate use of a quotation linking Islam and violence.[1]
More and more college courses on religion and violence have pro-
liferated over the last decade to meet student interest and demand.
These courses do not explore theodicy, such as theological reflections after the Holocaust; rather, they are exploring the nature of
resurgent religion as a violent force in modern society. You can add
to this a myriad of popular cultural despisers of religion making similar claims, such as Richard Dawkins, Sam Harris, and Christopher
Hitchens. Even scholarly works on the relationship between religion and violence have gained popular notice. Both Terry Gross and
Bill O'Reilly interviewed Wake Forest professor Charles Kimball,
author of *When Religion Becomes Evil*.[2] This book was also named
by *Publisher's Weekly* as the top religion book for 2002. Political
Scientist Benjamin R. Barber's *Jihad vs. McWorld* was a *New York
Times* Bestseller.[3] And Mark Juergensmeyer's *Terror in the Mind
of God* was named world expert's choice by the *Washington Post*.[4]
This collection of examples suggests that people are paying attention to religion, and especially to its violent manifestations.

Despite the boon such interest might have for religion departments jockeying for precious tenure lines, I feel uneasy about it,
partially because religion's new popularity seems to rest on the very
conflation that the historian assumed when he asked if I would kill
in the name of Christ, that religion is vital only when it is open to the
commission of violence. This conflation, I believe, helps undermine
Americans' ability to take religion seriously in the academy, in the
classroom, and in the public arena. I also believe that those of us
who research, teach, or promote proper religious engagement in our
society must challenge the academy and the culture to approach the
current popular interest of religious violence with suspicion, lest it
undermine each person's role as a scholar, a teacher, and a citizen.

Before I examine my specific objections, let me be frank.
My suspicion of, and worry about, the idea that violent religious
actions evidences vital religious faith comes from a commitment to
a Christian humanism. Of course, one need not be a Christian to be
a humanist, nor are all Christians committed humanists. However,
I would argue that a humanism that is Christian finds its foundation

in the doctrine of the incarnation. Since God became human, we recognize the inherent value of all human beings. Further, if humanity has God-given value, then the Christian in the academy should recognize that all things human and affecting humanity are worthy of study. Conversely, we must resist the temptation to dehumanize or dismiss someone or some human activity as "the other," implying that they are not worthy of fair investigation. The term "human" implies that, on a very basic level, there is the potential to understand someone else because we share a nature with that someone else. With the Roman poet Terence, the Christian humanist asserts that "I am human so nothing human is alien to me." In the end, a Christian in the academy studies human beings and human activities with fairness and charity, with an aim to see the truth about them as much as possible. All this is to say that the Christian humanist is not interested in religion simply because he or she is religious or believes in God; rather, religion also has importance because it is a human phenomenon.

Having given this far too brief sketch of Christian humanism, I would like to make a few modest observations about why I think the modern infatuation with religious violence hinders our ability to take religion seriously.

First, the scholar should be suspicious of the popular conflation of violent religion with vital religion in the absence of arguments and evidence supporting such a position. Neither the claim that religious vitality is best measured by violent actions, nor the claim that religion is inherently violent are self-evident. However, too often, these ideas are posited without reflection. I want to be clear: I am not suggesting that violent religious extremism does not exist. I am also not intimating that violence has not been done in the name of religion, or that it has not been justified by using genuine pieces of religious traditions. However, such admissions are not the same as creating a compelling case that vital religion is violent.

Theologian Miroslav Volf's distinction between "thin" and "thick" religion provides a helpful framework to show what would be needed to make a compelling claim that vital religion is necessarily open to violence.[5] Volf develops what he calls "thin" religion from Clifford Geertz's concept of "thin description," in which an ethnographer imputes meaning to observed actions, events, or symbols, all with little or no reference to the cultural systems that created them. According to Geertz, an ethnographer describes "thinly" when she attempts to understand some cultural activity out of context and without reference to the very culture, traditions, and communities in which it actually functions. Analogously, Volf argues that those who practice (and I would add, observe) religions "thinly" take certain ideas and practices of a religion and overemphasize or exaggerate them without reference to the tradition as a whole and as believed and practiced over time. The "thin" practitioner or observer, therefore, ultimately creates a caricature of the religion in question. Religion, in these cases, has not been taken seriously.[6]

Volf, however, suggests that truly vital faith is not "thin," but rather, "thick." According to him, practitioners of "thick" religion are truly engaged and serious about the faith they profess to believe, because they consult and engage their religion's full tradition over its history. In order to show that a violent action is the result of "thick" practice, one must show that such violence is a necessary result from a careful and broad engagement with the religious tradition in question by the majority of the adherents of the faith over its history. Admittedly, Volf does not make the strong claim that no violent religious actions are "thick." However, his distinction between thick and thin religion creates a burden of proof upon those who would simply posit that violent religion is vital religion. Further, simply observing that religious individuals have done violent acts throughout history does not adequately meet the burden of proof with a level of depth and sophistication that should satisfy scholarly inquiry over this question.

I would similarly assert that religion's inherent violence is not self-evident. I believe that William Cavanaugh has rightly argued that any claim of religion's inherent violence would need to show successfully that religion (rather than, say, emerging nationalism, economic interests, or personal lust for power) was uniquely decisive in a violent event or pattern of violence.[7] This would require, first, that a clear definition of religion be employed that does not assume religion's violence. More importantly, such a claim would need to take religion seriously by determining whether the violent act was "thinly" or "thickly" practiced in the manner described by Volf. Finally, one would also need to make a comparative study across history to see if, indeed, religion seemed to have a decisively violent nature. The onus to prove an argument remains with the arguers in this case, especially since all of us could provide a myriad of counterfactuals, like Jesus, Buddha, Gandhi, or King. Of course, I am not saying that such a study could not, in theory, be done; however, I have yet to see an argument made with a preponderance of evidence based upon a broad enough examination of the world's religious traditions to make such a general claim about "religion" compelling.[8] Anything less than such a study is anecdotal (or, worse, simply reflects the nightly news) and does not take religion seriously in a manner worthy of our academic communities.

Next, I think that the fixation on religious violence challenges our ability, as teachers, to take religion seriously in the classroom. It seems to me that this fixation is symptomatic of a culture that consumes violence and violent images to cure its boredom. Philip Rieff, in his classic *The Triumph of the Therapeutic*, noted that "a social structure shakes with violence and shivers with fear of violence not merely when that social structure is callously unjust but also when its members must stimulate themselves to feverish activity in order to demonstrate how alive they are."[9] If general members of our society feel "alive," as Rieff says, by participating in or watching violence, we educators feel alive when our students show interest of any kind in our subject. However, we cannot be satisfied with what I will call the "*Da Vinci Code* syndrome," which usually sounds something like this: "Well, Dan Brown may mislead people through a clever conflation of fact and fiction, but at least students are asking questions about these subjects for once." While I agree that any question is better than no questions, I also believe that teaching students to ask good questions is better than waiting for them to ask any old questions. I worry that we educators depend too much on popular interest generated by titillating current events, exaggeration of facts, or outright misinformation, hoping these things will bring our students to the academic discussion table. Instead, we must help students develop the skills to undertake the patient study by which they may interpret the world. I know this is idealistic and may never be fully realized; however, I have too much experience with students who, by simply aiming to pass a class, manage to fail it. In other words, lacking ideals is the surest way to never reach them (even for those occasional students who make teaching immediately worthwhile). Popularity is a fickle lover. Focusing on religious violence may draw students' interest, but the notice will be fleeting, and it will likely leave the learning shallow.

Finally, the conflation of religious vitality with violent religious extremism challenges the ability of our culture to take religion seriously in the public sphere. Insofar as the reason to study religion is tied to its violent manifestations in the modern world, it ultimately makes religion a civic problem that needs a cure, rather than a natural human endeavor that might contribute positively to society as a whole. Using the religion-is-violent thesis, the cultural despisers of faith argue that the vitality (and hence the danger) of any religion that proves itself resistant to the corrosive acids of modernity is its adherents' unwavering and unreasonable commitment to its own "truth." Enlightenment thinkers called this form of commitment "enthusiasm." Enthusiastic commitments that grant assent to beliefs not proved by the light of unaided reason provided the mythic explanation for the so-called "wars of religion" that ravaged Europe's population at the hands of Protestant or Catholic armies during the sixteenth and seventeenth centuries. According to such thinkers, one could avoid religion's deadly vitality by tempering one's assent to any religious proposition in proportion to its reasonableness. Perhaps not surprisingly, these thinkers wished to push traditional religious propositions from the category of truth and knowledge to the realm of private individuals and their opinions. Further, it was argued that the easiest way to save civil society from religion's enthusiastic potential was to extricate it from the public sphere. Those convinced by such a view would certainly find compelling one of my colleague's bumper stickers, which reads, "The last time we mixed church and state, people were burned at the stake."

By not challenging the conflation of religious vitality and violent religious extremism, we encourage individuals and societies either to exploit religion by attempting to harness the unbridled passion it supposedly possesses, or to neutralize it by privatizing or disenfranchising it. In the words of historian Elisabeth Lasch-Quinn, "Whenever it has any use of belief, our age presses religion into the service of power. The rest of the time it banishes faith from any position of authority."[10] Neither religion's manipulators nor its civilized detractors wish to see a full-fledged tradition engage the culture in which it resides. Its enthusiasm, they argue, is just too potent. Although much more should be said, let me simply state that the Christian humanist should not be satisfied with a view of religion that ultimately encourages the chaining of God's blessing to the service of the state or the barring of religious voices from the public sphere. The manipulator encourages misunderstanding in order to funnel religious vitality away from its divine focus. Religion's detractors seek to create a litmus test of disbelief in order to protect themselves from their own caricature of men and women of faith.

In the end, what is lost is the very positive role that religion might play to help our social ills or, perhaps, must play in a world plagued by "thin" religion. Vital faith, as de Tocqueville observed, has the potential to challenge our American materialism and individualism, which corrode our social fabric. Such religion demands that we feed the poor. It claims that, rather than consumers, we are human beings with more value than our credit line or checkbooks. It challenges the powerful by tending to the oppressed. A vitally religious person may even put his or her life on the line to expose injustice or protect the innocent. If we banish religion from the public sphere, we should rightfully wonder whether we will be able hear the call of the next Martin Luther King, Jr. or Dorothy Day. And wouldn't that be our loss and to our discredit? Further, if we banish religion from the public sphere, we banish those most able to expose "thin" religion and encourage "thick" religion in a world that is increasingly turning to religious resources to express their dissatisfaction with political injustice, social inequality, and economic disparity. In this sense, the real danger may be not taking religion seriously by refusing to engage it on its own terms. As R. Scott Appleby recently observed, the best hope for reducing violent religious extremism resides within those deeply committed to religion itself. "They would be," he suggests, "de facto cultural and religious ambassadors armed with the most essential tool in the diplomat's repertoire: insight."[11]

I have argued that, by focusing on violent manifestations of faith, members of our culture do not ultimately take religion seriously. Further, we have a duty as intellectually honest scholars to challenge "common wisdom" that conflates religious vitality and violent religious extremism with weak and anecdotal claims. Rather, we must demand arguments with compelling evidence. As teachers, we must encourage our students to value the patient search for truth about the nature of religion over the excitement of the titillating details we hear in news stories. And as citizens, we should be careful not to banish religious individuals or groups from the public sphere because of their faith. To do so will leave us with fewer motivated individuals to address the serious social, political, and economic ills facing our society and, worse, may leave us without representatives that would be most able to converse with those religious people we increasingly seem to fear and misunderstand in a post-9/11 world.

This chapter also appeared as an essay in *The Cresset* (Michaelmas 2007, pp. 6–10).

Endnotes

1. "Religious Newswriters Identify Year's Top Ten Religion Stories," *Religious Studies News* Vol. 22, No. 3 (May 2007): p. 11.

2. Charles Kimball, *When Religion Becomes Evil* (New York: HarperOne, 2002).

3. Benjamin R. Barber, *Jihad vs. McWorld* (New York: Crown, 1995).

4. Mark Juergensmeyer, *Terror in the Mind of God: The Global Rise of Religious Violence*. (Berkeley, CA: University of California Press, 2000). See: David B. Edwards, "Expert's Picks; Afghanistan," *Washington Post*, November 11, 2001.

5. Miroslav Volf, "Christianity and Violence," Boardman Lectureship in Christian Ethics, Boardman Lecture XXXVIII, University of Pennsylvania Department of Religious Studies, Adam Graves, ed., March 1, 2002. (repository. upenn.edu/boardman/2)

6. Volf discusses practice, not observation; however, I believe his use of Geertz could be applied to observers, as well as practitioners.

7. William Cavanaugh, "The Violence of 'Religion': Examining a Prevalent Myth," Kellogg Institute for International Studies Working Papers, No. 310 (Notre Dame, IN: University of Notre Dame, March 2004).

8. Some studies have been done on monotheistic faiths, although they, too, have been seriously criticized, obviously suggesting that such arguments are not self-evident. For a recent example, see Robert Gnuse, "Breakthrough or Tyranny: Monotheism's Contested Implications," *Horizons* Vol. 34, No. 1 (Spring 2007): pp. 78–95.

9. Philip Rieff, *The Triumph of the Therapeutic: Uses of Faith after Freud* (Wilmington, DE: ISI, 2006), p. 8.

10. Quoted in Rieff, p. vii.

11. R. Scott Appleby, "A Radical Solution." *Foreign Policy*, No. 160 (May/June 2007): p. 40.

The Christian Academic
and the Church

CHAPTER EIGHT

Have Women Souls?

The Council of Mâcon and the Dilemma
of a Catholic Feminist Scholar

Kathleen Sprows Cummings

In June 1905, in the proud tradition of commencement speakers everywhere, Henry Edmunds made a remark at the Philadelphia Girls' High School graduation ceremony that he would later regret: Edmunds, the president of the city's Board of Education, observed that "Woman has always been unfairly discriminated against by man … Even as late as the fifteenth century there was held in the south of France a council of learned prelates who for two days discussed the question of whether woman had a soul or not."[1] Surprised, several Catholic members of the audience demanded that Edmunds name the council and produce a source. After some equivocation, he cited *Sketches on the Old Road through France to Florence*, a book published a year earlier by the artist A. H. Hallam Murray. According to Murray, the debate had actually taken place in the sixth century, during the Council at Mâcon in the South of France: "The question before the Council was whether women had souls. That point was left open, but the subsidiary dogma was fixed forever, and since that Council in the middle of the sixth century it has been quite possible to remain a good Catholic and yet to doubt…. that women are practically of the same species as ourselves."[2]

71

This reference did little to placate Rev. Philip McDevitt, the Superintendent of Schools for the Archdiocese of Philadelphia and an indefatigable Catholic apologist. Subjecting the official decrees of Mâcon to careful scrutiny, McDevitt found no references to the alleged debate. He did discover in the notes to the Council an account of a quibble over terminology that he believed was "the only possible thing that could be distorted into the calumny" Murray and others would later allege. McDevitt explained it in detail: "The note states that there was at the Council a certain bishop who said that 'woman' could not be called 'man:' *Extit enim in hac synodo, quidam ex episcopis, qui dicebat mulierem hominem non posse vocari.*"[3] It was likely, McDevitt explained, "that the bishop's knowledge of Latin was limited and that he did not know that *homo*, the generic term, could be applied to *mulier*, 'woman,' as well as to *vir*, 'man.'" Subsequent chroniclers of Mâcon, determined to present the Church in a bad light, had transformed confusion over grammar into a debate over dogma. "From this trifling incident," McDevitt noted, "occasioned by one bishop not unduly equipped with a knowledge of Latin terms, the Council of Mâcon is made to discuss for two days whether woman had a soul."[4]

According to McDevitt, this "gross distortion" was all too typical when Protestant writers reported "facts" about the Catholic Church. "Nothing," he lamented, "is too small or improbable for people with preconceived antipathies to represent the Catholic Church as issuing palpably absurd pronouncements."[5] In this case, this misrepresentation was particularly insulting, considering that it completely "contradicted the belief and practice of the Catholic Church in regard to women."[6]

Whether or not McDevitt's rebuttal elicited a *mea culpa* from Edmunds is unknown, but he undoubtedly could have deflected much of the blame for his error by pointing to a number of other sources that corroborated Murray's account. In 1879, August Bebel had described in *Woman and Socialism* how the bishops of Mâcon "indulged in a serious discussion as to whether woman had a soul, and finally decided in her favor by a majority of one." The Council of Mâcon, Bebel argued, "disproved the claim that Christianity was favorable to woman."[7] In 1893, Matilde Joslyn Gage cited the meeting at Mâcon as evidence of the misogyny of the Church in her critique of patriarchal religion, *Woman, Church and State*.[8] Given her belief that "the repression of women was one of the principal *functions* of churches," it is hardly surprising to find Gage repeating the fabled account of Mâcon. But it also surfaced within mainstream Christian denominations. Writing in the *Gospel Advocate* in 1896, Mrs. T. P. Holman wondered, "Is there a New Woman, and if so, What Causes Led to Her Creation?" To consider the question properly, Holman maintained, it was necessary to consider how women were treated in the remote past: "The position of woman in the past ages has been a low one," she declared. "In A.D. 585, a solemn ecclesiastical council was held at Mâcon for the purpose of determining whether or not women had a soul."[9]

McDevitt's efforts at rebuttal were to no avail. A year later, a Cornell professor repeated the account during a public lecture on the education of women in France, noting that "one of the Church councils had even discussed the question as to whether women had souls or not and had arrived at a negative conclusion." Writing in the *North American Review* in 1915, Lawrence Gilman praised the recent progress of "Woman—once despised—woman—to whom at the Council of Mâcon a soul had been denied." Later that year, a writer in the *Atlantic Monthly* cited the debate at Mâcon an example of men's tendency to deny women's intellect. Accounts of the alleged challenge to women's souls at Mâcon would appear elsewhere, although the council in question was alternately identified as Nicaea, Trent, or an unspecified "ecumenical council of the Middle Ages."[10]

McDevitt and others would continue to labor mightily, though in vain, to lay the legend of Mâcon to rest. One priest had predicted in 1906 that the apocryphal "have women souls" debate would never die, because "The story is too good and will go on developing. The controversialist, the evolutionist, the after-dinner wit, the educational reformer, the woman suffragist, all will appeal to some mythical Church council, deliberating for weeks or months in any century before Luther and liberty…"[11] Indeed, the specter of Mâcon haunts Roman Catholics to this day, despite the fact that the myth has since been debunked in far greater detail than McDevitt did a century ago. To my mind, this has been done quite convincingly by Michael Nolan in a recent article that appeared in *First Things*.[12] Alas, "Ms. Mentor," an advice columnist for the *Chronicle of Higher Education*, must not be an avid reader of *First Things*, as she recently offered her opinion of committee work for the benefit of a beleaguered assistant professor: "Ms. Mentor does not thoroughly disdain committee work. She knows that she would enjoy the literate and somber deliberation of, say, a Nobel Prize Committee.... But she would shun the Council of Mâcon (585 AD) at which a committee of bishops [allegedly] debated whether women had souls." [13]

Though some would attribute the periodic surfacing of the Mâcon myth to the lingering presence of anti-Catholicism in the United States, I would argue there is a much more precise and more convincing explanation: Then and now, the deliberations at Mâcon simply do not appear as implausible to outsiders as defenders of the Church would like to believe. While there is no question that exaggeration and misunderstanding have exacerbated the problem, the Catholic Church became the *bête noire* of the "woman suffragist" and the contemporary secular feminist for good reason. As one early twentieth-century subscriber to the Mâcon myth mused, it had "never occurred to the Council to discuss whether man had a soul, possibly because all its members were men."[14] And therein lies the problem: Given the Church's patriarchal structure, it is hardly beyond the pale to believe that some of its leaders could once have questioned women's soulful humanity. While the Catholic Church has never denied women a soul, it has played a key role in perpetuating an ideology of gender that reinforces women's status as inferior to men.

I recount this strange history of Mâcon because it provides an opening to reflect upon the dilemma of being both a scholar who is influenced and persuaded by feminism and a member of a religious tradition in which leadership and power structures remain unrelentingly and unapologetically dominated by men. As a member of two groups who are reflexively inclined to believe the worst about each other, I often find myself in an uncomfortable position:

Often, one of my sister or fellow Catholics imply (or even state out-right) that though—thankfully—I do not appear to be as angry or as crazy as most of them, I am still tainted by my association with feminists; on the other hand, I get the distinct sense that most of my colleagues in women's studies believe that, by continuing to profess the Catholic faith, I am undoubtedly, though perhaps unwittingly, complicit in my own oppression.

At times, those tensions are brought into particularly sharp relief. A few years ago, the Catholic university where I teach was embroiled in a debate about whether to allow *The Vagina Monologues* to be performed on campus. For weeks, the story made headlines in newspapers throughout the country. One day, in the middle of the controversy, my father called me at my office to report gleefully that the pastor of his parish had prayed from the pulpit that God bless Notre Dame's efforts to "save Catholic higher education" from feminists and liberals. (This was the same parish where an assistant pastor had once commented to me, "Oh, Notre Dame. Don't you all use gender-neutral language there? That's diabolical, you know. *From the devil…*" he clarified, in case I didn't understand).

Not long after I hung up the phone with my dad that after-noon, I dashed to a hastily-organized meeting of women faculty. Among the many concerns expressed there was the fear that this controversy was merely one more way that a Catholic institution was seeking to marginalize women's power and minimize women's issues. As one of a handful of publicly-identified Catholic women present, it was hard not to feel that I was implicitly associated with the enemy.

But these are the worst moments. In my best moments, it has also been possible for me to hold what seem to be dueling identi-ties in creative tension. My familiarity with Catholic tradition has often yielded fresh insights into the history of American women, just as my criticism of the Catholic Church has offered a new lens on its history in the United States. The "have women souls" debate is one such instance: In my larger study of gender and American Catholicism in the Progressive era, I have argued that the legend of Mâcon provides important context for understanding how U.S. Catholics relied on a gendered past to define and defend themselves as American citizens. Throughout the early twentieth century, Rev. McDevitt and other Catholics blamed the recurrence of the Mâcon myth on the pervasive influence of the growing women's suffrage movement. Suffragists, they believed, were at the vanguard of a conspiracy designed to paint the Catholic Church as the historic and ongoing oppressor of women. And they were not being entirely paranoid: As more women with wealth, status, and privilege joined the cause in the early twentieth century, the case for suffrage increasingly rested on the argument that, if African-American, uneducated, or "foreign" men were able to vote, then white, middle-class women surely deserved the franchise. While the racial and class biases of the suffragists are widely acknowledged by historians, scholars have paid little attention to the significance of the fact that the majority of the uneducated and foreign "undesirables" were Catholic.[15]

But, as the editors of *America Magazine* noted in 1915, if "some suffragist, impatient of Romish conservatism," could whisper the account of Mâcon into "guileless ears," Catholics could respond in kind, pointing to a host of female figures from the past that testified to the way Christianity had served as the historic emancipator of women. This fact alone did not distinguish them from leaders in other religious denominations, but very telling was the preponderance of heroines that Catholics produced from the sixteenth and seventeenth centuries. The timing, of course, was auspicious. The fact that so many pious and accomplished women "graced the Church in the first hundred years after the birth of Protestantism," underscored an important corollary to the proposition that Christianity had liberated women: it was Catholics, not Protestants, who had emerged from the Reformation divide as the proper heirs to Christianity's historic role as the protector of women's rights.[16] Catholic women made this argument, as well. Margaret Sullivan pointed to Jane de Chantal and other founders of religious congregations to highlight "the undeniable fact that Protestantism has never been able permanently to maintain a single community of women." This failure, she argued, "proves that the *Catholic Church alone* is the sphere in which woman's religious zeal finds its fullest and most complete expression; that it is *the Catholic faith alone* which thoroughly arouses and solidly supports the enthusiasm of her nature, and embodies her ardor into a useful and enduring form."[17] Essayist Agnes Repplier made a similar argument about the seventeenth-century French missionary Marie l'Incarnation. Though faced with daunting obstacles, Marie "stamped herself firmly upon the history of the Church … She did not destroy what she undertook to reform, which is always an easy thing to do."[18]

Contained within these accounts was an unmistakable message sent to Catholic women: Their loyalties were better placed with the Church than foolish and misguided women's rights advocates, who were irreligious or, perhaps even worse, Protestant. This campaign enjoyed spectacular success, as Catholic women collectively evinced little enthusiasm for suffrage or what they viewed as its "ugly attendant," feminism. The seeds of gender discontent would lay dormant until the 1960s, when, watered by the Second Vatican Council, massive social change in American society, and significant demographic change, Catholic women would respond much differently to feminism in its second wave.

The classroom is another place where I attempt to bridge the chasm that often separates feminist and Catholic scholars. I regularly teach a course on the history of Women and American Catholicism, and of the students who enroll in it, about two-thirds are devout Catholics whom I would generally characterize as "conservative" with regard to gender and the Church. They are skeptical, if not explicitly hostile, toward feminism; if they have considered women's ordination (most have not), they are opposed to it. Increasingly, many of them are well-versed in, and persuaded by, the theology of Pope John Paul II, especially the "new feminism." Much of its language of "complementarity" evokes the traditional Church teaching that women are defined relative to men and through their self-sacrificial role within the family. In this respect, the new feminism bears an uncanny resemblance to the old "anti-feminism," and it certainly does not fit the definition of feminism which I accept and use.

For the record, I borrow my definition from Stanford professor Estelle Freedman's well-regarded *No Turning Back: The History of Feminism and the Future of Women.* This definition of feminism would be readily accepted by any person who takes feminism seriously, and it has three components: First, feminists believe that men and women are inherently of equal worth. Second, feminists seek to accommodate innate sexual difference—biological differences between men and women—but to dismantle historically contingent, and thus inessential differences of gender, which are defined as the meanings that society attaches to biological differences. Third, feminists recognize that oppression based on gender is intertwined with other forms of oppression, such as those based on race or class.

Approximately one-third of my students would self-identify as feminists. While most members of this contingent are also Catholic, they tend to be more critical of the Church. On the first day of class last fall, one of the members of this group announced that she had signed up for the course simply out of curiosity: "How," she demanded, "can a course on Women and Catholicism last any longer than *two weeks*?" Given women's absence from power structures within the Roman Catholic Church, she wondered, what could we possibly find to talk about for an entire semester?

At the very least, the combination of these two groups assures that we have interesting conversations. At best, members of this group move closer together as the semester progresses. Last fall, one of the ways I tried to facilitate this development was by capitalizing on a happy coincidence. In mid-semester, Mother Theodore Guerin, the founder of the Sisters of Providence in Terre Haute, Indiana, was canonized as the eighth American saint and the very first from Indiana! I incorporated this event as much as possible into the class. I invited her vice-postulator (the member of the community who was in charge of the canonization) to speak to the class, and I assigned some of her correspondence, most of which related to Guerin's power struggles with Celestine de la Hailandière, the bishop of Vincennes. Hailandière's repeated challenges to Guerin's authority over community matters culminated in 1847, when he locked Guerin in his house until she acceded to his demands. A day later, he removed her as superior, released her from religious vows, and threatened her and any sisters who followed her with excommunication. Guerin resolved to start over in the diocese of Detroit, where she was assured of a warm welcome. But in what was surely providential timing, word arrived from Rome that Hailandière had been replaced as Bishop of Vincennes. The Sisters of Providence stayed and flourished under the new bishop, and today, their 465 members work in ten states, the District of Colombia, China, and Taiwan. Reflecting on Guerin's canonization in a *New York Times* op-ed that appeared on All Saints Day, 2007, Rev. James Martin wondered "what Bishop Hailandière thinks from his post in heaven—or wherever he is today."[19]

For the more traditional students, hearing about Guerin's struggle with a clerical superior complicated their understanding of what being a "good Catholic woman" means, and they became a bit less inclined to dismiss feminist arguments. Students in the latter group, meanwhile, interpreted Guerin's resourcefulness and faithfulness as evidence that women have always found sources of power within this male-dominated institution. These and other experiences in the classroom, particularly with young Catholic women, have led me to believe that, as a historian of women and feminism, I can help to fulfill what Richard Yanikoski recently described as his hope that "a more pronounced prophetic voice will become one of Catholic higher education's distinctive contributions to the world." Yanikoski, president of the Association of Catholic Colleges and Universities, has written eloquently about how this prophetic voice can lead to "institutional or personal actions that in a penetrating manner call attention to serious worldly problems and seek to redress them in ways consistent with Christ's teaching."[20] As inspiring as I find that, I also have a hope that scholars can serve as a similar prophetic voice *within* the Church, as we envision a day when the fabled account of Mâcon is universally recognized as the absurdity it is, and when people no longer ask me how it is possible to be both Catholic and a feminist, but wonder, instead, how it is possible to be a Catholic and *not* be one.

An expanded version of this essay appeared as an article in *Commonweal* ("Do Women Have Souls?" September 11, 2009).

Endnotes

1. Rev. Philip McDevitt, "Boards of Education and Historical Truth: 'Chiefly Among Women' by Mrs. Margaret Sullivan," *Educational Briefs* 13 (1906): p. 4. See original in "Notes on "Have Women Souls?," Box 5, folder 33, Philip McDevitt Papers, (CMCD), University of Notre Dame Archives, Notre Dame, IN (UNDA).

2. Quoted in McDevitt, "Boards of Education," p. 5.

3. Translation of the first sentence, "For there stood up in this synod a certain man among the Bishops who said, that a woman was not able to be called a human." The remainder of the passage reads "But still he was satisfied with the rationale accepted by the Bishops: that which says, that where the Old Testament of the Holy Bible teaches, that in the beginning, there was man from God the Creator; male and female he created them, and called them Adam because he is a human from the earth; and so from there calling them woman or man: for he said that both are human. But also Our Lord Jesus is called, according to this [the Bible], the son of man, because he is the son of a virgin, which is to say the son of a woman, and with this argument of his refuted by many other testimonies the man was satisfied."

4. McDevitt, "Boards of Education," p. 7.

5. Ibid., p. 7.

6. Ibid., p. 3.

7. August Bebel, *Woman and Socialism*, www.marxists.org/archive/bebel/1879/woman-socialism/ch03.html

8. Matilda Joslyn Gage, *Woman, Church and State: A Historical Account of the Status of Woman through the Christian Ages with Reminiscences of the Matriarchate* (1893), p. 56.

9. Mrs. T.P. Holman, "The 'New Woman'" *Gospel Advocate*, July 9 1896, p. 438.

10. Rev. F.P. Donnelly, SJ "Have Women Souls?" *The Messenger* (March 1906): p. 302; Lawrence Gilman, "A History of Love," *North American Review* 201 (1915): p. 910; W. L. George, "Notes on the Intelligence of Woman," *Atlantic Monthly* (December 1915) ; See also "Catholic Apologetics—Historical Myths; Letters to Newspapers re: Misstatements," Box 5, folder 24, CMCD, NDA. This folder contains a clipping of an article from the October 26, 1922, *New York Evening World* that referred to it as Nicaea, as well as a copy of a letter from Edward Walsh to the Editor of the *Ecclesiastical Review*, June 8, 1916, which reports a reference to the debate at Trent, in "Notes to Have Women Souls," CMCD; "Has a Council Denied that Women Have Souls," *The Fortnightly Review* 22 (1915): pp. 742–743.

11. Donnelly, "Have Women Souls?" p. 304.

12. Michael Nolan, "The Myth of Soulless Women," *First Things* 72 (April 1997): 13-14.

13. "Fear of Committee-ment," *Chronicle of Higher Education*, November 16, 2001.

14. George, "Notes on Intelligence of Woman."

15. Sara M. Evans, *Born for Liberty: A History of Women in America* (Free Press, 1997), 155–156; Louise Michele Newman, *White Woman's Rights: The Racial Origins of Feminism in the United States* (New York: Oxford, 1999).

16. Rev. Joseph McSorely, SJ, "Saint Chantal: A Type of Christian Womanhood," *Catholic World* 76 (1903): 572–573.

17. Margaret Buchanan Sullivan, "Chiefly among Women," *Catholic World* (1875): 332. Emphasis added.

18. Agnes Repplier, *Mère Marie of the Ursulines: A Study in Adventure* (Garden City, NY: Country Life Press, 1931), p. 286.

19. James Martin, "Saints that Weren't," *New York Times*, November 1, 2007.

20. Richard Yanikoski, "The Prophetic Voice of Catholic Higher Education," *Origins: CNS Documentary Service* 36 (April 12, 2007), pp. 700–707.

CHAPTER NINE

The Professor in the Parish

Beyond Gourmet Coffee and
High-Quality Handouts

Martha Greene Eads

T he *Book of Common Prayer's* Proper for the Sunday closest
    to June 8 (the day this talk was delivered) in the Season of
    Pentecost, reads: "O God, from whom all good proceeds:
Grant that by your inspiration we may think these those things that
are right, and by your merciful guiding may do them; through Jesus
Christ our Lord, who lives and reigns with you and Holy Spirit,
one God, for ever and ever. *Amen.*"[1] What *are* these things that are
right for us to think, and subsequently, to do? The Eucharistic pref-
ace for Pentecost, also from the *Book of Common Prayer*, assures
us that the Holy Spirit came down from heaven and lit "upon the
disciples to teach them and lead them into all truth; uniting peoples of many tongues in the confession of one faith, and giving to
[God's] Church the power to serve [God] as a royal priesthood, and
to preach the Gospel to all nations."[2] As professors, we aspire to
find and promote the lower-case "t"-truths within our disciplines;
professionally, we care about truth-telling. As those who profess
faith in Christ, however, we also claim access to the capital "T"-
Truth that the disciples learned and taught as a result of Pentecost,
a Truth that unites diverse people in the church, equipping them to

83

serve God and to preach the Gospel. And that, as we all know, is the Bible's focus—far more than the truths of any of our disciplines. As Stanley Hauerwas so frequently points out, Scripture reveals the story of God's work to redeem the world, first through Israel, and then more expansively through the church.

Those of us who obsess about scholarship and teaching as our vocation may be disturbed to discover that very few of the players in the drama of Scripture held *jobs* that contributed significantly to God's plot's unfolding. David's having been a shepherd and a king has made a difference to believers throughout the centuries, and Esther's being a member of Xerxes's harem (if we want to think of *that* as a job) made a difference, but did Paul's being a tent-maker, or Lydia's being a textiles dealer, or even Jesus' supposedly being a carpenter? For most of us, our being professors (or nurses, or music teachers, or family therapists, or stay-at-home parents) makes sense only within relatively short scenes of the already millennia-long divine drama. In the great scheme of things, I suspect, "these things that are right" that we ought to think include the Truth that our being in the church matters more than our being in the academy. And we enter the church through our local congregations, as Hauerwas and his good friend William Willimon remind us. They point out in *Lord, Teach Us*, "There may be religions that come to you through quiet walks in the woods, or by sitting quietly in the library with a book, or rummaging around in the recesses of your psyche. Christianity is not one of them. Christianity is inherently communal, a matter of life in the Body, the Church."[3]

We find Scriptural evidence for the greater importance of congregational identity than individual vocational identity in Acts, where we read about Barnabas, whose feast day many Christians celebrate at this point in the church calendar. Chapter 13 tells us: "In the church at Antioch there were prophets and teachers: Barnabas, Simeon called Niger, Lucius of Cyrene, Maneaen (who had been brought up with Herod the tetrarch) and Saul." We don't know what these people did, beyond their roles as prophets and teachers within their congregation. What we do know is the effect of Barnabas's participation in his congregation and, later, in the wider church. Acts 11:23–24 tells us, "When he arrived [at Antioch] and saw the evidence of the grace of God, he was glad and encouraged them all to remain true to the Lord with all their hearts. He was a good man, full of the Holy Spirit and faith, and a great number of people were brought to the Lord."

To gather further insight on the role that academics might play in the church, I posed the following question to clergy-friends of mine from several traditions: "What do you wish scholar-teachers would bring to your church?" One of these friends, Frederica Mathewes-Green, offered counsel consistent with this example of a saint whose character and witness are far more memorable than whatever work he did. An Antiochian Orthodox writer and teacher, Frederica also serves alongside her husband as the *khoria*, or spiritual "mother," in their Baltimore, Maryland, congregation. After asking for a few days to think about the subject of the scholar's role in the church, Frederica replied somewhat apologetically, writing,

> I'm afraid I'm not coming up with anything original! I asked some Orthodox pastors, too. It's admirable that scholars would want to be useful in their local congregations, but how to take up that offer depends, I suppose, on what special expertise they bring; an architecture professor would be helpful in ways different from a history professor …What I and Orthodox pastors would say we most want a scholar to be is holy; to be a person who is on a path of transformation in Christ, earnestly seeking gifts of humility, generosity, and love. If that, or at least the desire for that, is in place, the application of more practical areas of expertise will surface naturally.[4]

Another friend, Dan Woods, wrote more bluntly, but his response, too, underscores the limited value and even the potential dangers of having a congregation full of academics. A bi-vocational Pentecostal pastor in southern Virginia, Dan also teaches history at a small Methodist college, Ferrum, where he co-led a National Endowment for the Humanities seminar I attended in 2004. Dan's intellect, sense of humor, and challenging yet down-to-earth teaching style made him a favorite among my NEH cohort that year, even among those who were hostile to Christian faith. Watching and hearing Dan's winsome witness that summer came to mean more to me than the scholarly insights I gained or the professional contacts I made, which were considerable. I was eager, then, in preparing for this talk, to hear what Dan wants from scholars in his congregation. In response to my question, he wrote,

> I will be praying for you, Sister Marti. This is a great topic and opportunity. I am "twixt & tween" on this one. I have pastored a small church or served as an associate in a large church most of my twenty-six years as a professor at Ferrum College. So I could speak out of both sides of my mouth without being duplicitous. A few godly professors are, I think, good for a church that might otherwise dismiss over-educated "posthole diggers" as without value. And these professors need to see in that church context that the gift of teaching spiritual matters may come upon saints who would never have qualified for admission as students to their distinguished institutions. A healthy, creative church, I believe, reflects the entire spectrum of any community (age, education, ethnicity, class, etc).

> One more thought: Too many professors can lead to a critical, even haughty, spirit that accomplishes little (but is quite pleased with itself in the process). Their greatest assets are the quality of their coffee and handouts.[5]

You have probably noted that Dan's admonition about professorial snobbery yielded the title for this reflection. His message left me wondering what I bring my congregation, Christ the King Episcopal Church—beyond certain cultivated aesthetic sensibilities. I had to chuckle, if ruefully, at his e-mail, thinking about the attitude with which I sometimes size up programs and practices in our year-and-a-half-old church plant. I sniff, for example, at most of our PowerPoint praise songs, and not until I saw how such music moves Marielle, my beloved eight-year-old fellow parishioner with developmental delays, did I acknowledge their value. In the hope of being more constructive, I've been serving on the liturgy team instead of just griping on the drive home from church each week. I've talked with our priest and music leader about one song with serious grammatical problems, but I am trying to be open to different musical styles for the sake of those whose understanding of worship differs from mine. Like Barnabas in Acts, I do see "evidence of the grace of God in" our congregation. Now, I need to be like him and "be glad," instead of nit-picking so much!

Another pastor-friend of mine, Masayuki Sawa of Fukuoka, Japan, shares Dan's concern about the potential for arrogance among professorial parishioners. Yuki served as my counselor during a high school American Field Service summer exchange to Japan in 1982, and we met again for the first time last year when I traveled to Japan to recruit for Eastern Mennonite University (EMU). I was surprised to find that most of the adults in his Reformed Church of Christ in Japan congregation were faculty or faculty spouses. In our recent e-mail exchange, Yuki wrote:

> I have more than ten scholars in our church now. Their fields of study differ from natural science such as biology, medicine, geology etc. to social science and literature, Japanese and English as well. One of them is teaching Christianity in a college.

> They are the specialists in their respected fields of study, just as a pastor has received a specialized discipline in theology. So a pastor and the scholar members can share a mutual respect as scholars. They expect me to be conscientious in my biblical and theological studies. I have to be humble, trying not to betray their expectations. So blessed is a pastor who has many scholars in the congregation, because he should become humble and keep learning!

But basically, there is neither Jew nor Greek, neither male nor female in Christ. So is there neither scholar nor non-scholar in the church of Christ. On the contrary, God chose what is low and despised, even things that are not, to bring nothing the things that are so that no human beings might boast in the presence of God.

So I should say, about what I wish the scholars in the congregations do to support the church in the negative way. To give testimony that it is not by their knowledge nor ability as scholars but by their modesty and faith that they can edify the Christian community.

You will sense the influence of the early theology of Karl Barth, his cry of "Nein!" among us.[6]

Yuki's suspicion of intellectual hierarchy within Christian congregations is striking in his Japanese context, where most people are profoundly conscious of social stratification. His perspective resonates, however, with that of the Mennonites with whom I now live and work. One prominent Mennonite scholar of the mid-twentieth century, J. C. Wenger, asserts:

The Christian view of the church is that it is not a hierarchy, but a brotherhood. We have one Master, even Christ, and we are all brethren … Let us be content to address one another in the Christian Church as Brother or Sister, rather than as Bishop, Reverend, Doctor, or Professor. There is no place for titles in the church of Christ.[7] (108)

In keeping with this conviction, EMU faculty, staff, and students have never used academic titles. In the institution's early years, community members addressed each other as Dan Woods addressed me in his e-mail—Sister Marti. Today at EMU, we're all on a first-name basis—even the university president. (Of course, his last name is Swartzendruber, so this practice obviously simplifies campus interactions!)

Y ou've probably noted that I've shifted here from discussing the congregation to discussing the campus. I must confess that this shift, or blurring, is the tension within today's talk and one of the central tensions in my life. This is where I'm at a loss in asking God for inspiration to "think these those things that are right, and by [His] merciful guiding [to] do them." I really do think that my primary allegiance needs to be to the church, rather than to the academy, but how does that play out when my university is owned and run by the Mennonite Church USA? Even if I worship most of the time in an Episcopal congregation, I am *passionate* about advancing Mennonite higher education. I often feel as if my service activities at EMU should "count" in the way that teaching Sunday school or being on the music team at Christ the King would "count." But I'm only a substitute Sunday school teacher, and I'm definitely not on the music team. The two women with whom I meet for prayer are EMU colleagues in the seminary and the nursing department, and the small group in which my husband and I participate is made up of those women, their husbands, and another academic couple. Despite a congregational expectation, I don't have a prayer partner at Christ the King, and aside from a delightful and less-hectic-than-usual period last summer, my husband and I haven't been in one of our congregation's small groups. I sometimes feel guilty about our choices.

Probably because of that guilt, I was surprised that Yuki revealed no such expectations of his congregants. In offering a positive counterpart to his Barthian "No," Yuki wrote, "What about the positive support and contribution to the church by the scholar members? I would expect them to work as Christians in the society. That is how they support the church as she exists in the world. As for their work in the church, I have not thought about it, so far."[8] When I wrote, incredulous, for confirmation, Yuki replied,

> Having read your mail, I gradually come to understand what the main point of your question is.

I have sympathy with you. Dr. Hesselink, former missionary to Japan and the president of the Western Theological Seminary in Holland, Michigan, once gave us a very interesting remark about the Japanese churches. He said, "It seems to me there is another loyalty other than the loyalty to Christ in Japanese churches. That is the loyalty to the church." As you probably know, there is a tendency of making "group" among the Japanese society. Like Toyota company, it is not only an enterprise but also a community for which a person lives and dies. [Dr. Hesselink] felt uncomfortable to see the Japanese Christians tended to stress too much the loyalty to the church as a group of people. Of course church exists as church visible on earth. But such "church visible" should always be relativized.[9]

Initially, Yuki's response comforted me. I read it as permission to be less involved in my congregation than I sometimes suspect I ought. Then, I wondered: Is the problem Dr. Hesselink describes among the Japanese common in our more individualistic North American culture, or do Japanese and U.S. Christians need to meet in the middle somewhere?

Once again, I look for counsel to Stanley Hauerwas. While he and Will Willimon point out that "the church is not … just the grinning folk who greet you at the door on Sunday morning at St. John's on the Expressway, but also the saints from every age and place who lead you in prayer," they nevertheless describe the church as the "visible, political enactment of our language of God by a people who can name their sin and accept God's forgiveness and are thereby enabled to speak the truth in love."[10] They assert that "[o]ur Sunday worship has a way of reminding us, in the most explicit and ecclesial of ways, of the source of our power, the peculiar nature of our solutions to what ails the world."[11] For Hauerwas, that visible and political enactment necessitates deep investment— so deep that when Duke University offered him a plummy teaching position, he sought permission from his South Bend, Indiana, congregation to resign his job at Notre Dame and move to North Carolina.

I need to ask Yuki whether his Japanese flock would be open to that kind of submission to those with whom they gather every Sunday; I know I would struggle with it. But in an effort to avoid standing here as a hypocrite—telling you that our primary allegiance and even submission must be to our local congregations, where our identity as scholar-teachers is secondary, at best—I scheduled an appointment with my own priest, Geoff Gwynne. A cradle Episcopalian, Geoff also had an adult conversion experience and leads our church plant with a missionary's zeal. I had posed the same e-mail question to him that I had sent to Dan and Yuki, and he had replied at some length along similar lines about the risk of scholars' being overly critical congregants. Writing about common traps for those with extensive formal education, including himself, Geoff wrote,

> [W]e sometimes … can be above certain things; we can think common obligations don't apply to us; we can be cynical and bring others down with us; we can be non-participant observers forever and decrease other's level of involvement; we can stay in our minds and not let our hands get dirty with ministry; we can use our learning to some divisive end; we can use words as defenses against criticism.[12]

When we met over coffee, though, Geoff, like Yuki, offered a "Yes" along with his "No." He noted, for example, that most scholars are adept at objective analysis, which can be quite helpful in explaining doctrine and liturgical practice, or in working through conflict. Moreover, in most congregations (Episcopalian, at least), scholarly credentials bring credibility, also useful for leadership. Like Frederica, though, Geoff believes that pursuing Christian maturity is far more important than bringing any particular skill set to the congregation. Taking seriously my charge to address this topic, Geoff said, "I would ask you to challenge your audience to meet with their pastors and ask for help in thinking about whether they're doing all they can for the Lord."[13]

Geoff made one other request that brings us full circle. Having written in our initial e-mail exchange:

> For me, and this is a very personal thought, there are few things under heaven as meaningful than hearing someone I respect say something encouraging. Many Sundays go by when many pastors hear nothing of personal encouragement. Absolute, or near absolute silence for the pastor is something every scholar can help, when circumstances merit some kind of measured praise. And there are few persons whose words would go further in the ears and heart of a pastor than that of the academically astute professor.[14]

Geoff's vulnerability in sharing this longing reminds us that our congregations, like the early church in Antioch, still need people like Barnabas, who, upon seeing "the evidence of the grace of God, ... was glad and encouraged them all."

So, as we reflect on the examples and teachings of Sister Frederica and Brothers Barnabas, Stanley, Dan, Yuki, and Geoff, perhaps we can return to our congregations thinking less about our roles as professors, and more about our pursuit of holiness, humility, generosity, and love. Those of us who complain about the fellowship hour's watery coffee (or, in my case, vapid song lyrics!) need to encourage the hospitality team and the music leader, even as we, from time to time, bring in freshly ground fair-trade Ethiopian Full City Roast or try to gently explain why switching among "you" and "thee" and "thou" in the same praise song is confusing.

And finally, let's commit to prioritizing worshiping weekly in our congregations, although that might mean making some professional sacrifices. Hauerwas and Willimon challenge us:

> [T]o say that Christians are those who always go to church on Sundays may be a more significant practice than we know.... In a world where work is integral to worth, where the majority of our neighbors see

Sunday morning as a time to go to the lake or to mow their grass, just getting up, getting dressed, and going to church becomes a sort of nonviolent protest, a way of saying, "We want a different world than the one you serve."[15]

In corresponding with Dan Woods about this reflection, I wrote, "I'm a little chagrined that this conference panel will take place on a Sunday morning when we all ought to be in church somewhere rather than in an academic ghetto. Dare I say that? (And still take my honorarium?)" He replied to each question in all caps, "ABSOLUTELY!"[16]

When I am next in church on a Sunday morning, Geoff will likely dismiss us by saying, "Go in peace to love and serve the Lord." That is an appropriate charge to us all as we continue seeking inspiration to "think these things that are right" and "by [God's] merciful guiding [to] do them." With this challenge in mind, let us close with one more prayer, that for the feast of Saint Barnabas:

> Grant, O Lord, that we may follow the example of your faithful servant Barnabas, who seeking not his own renown but the well-being of your Church, gave generously of his life and substance for the relief of the poor and the spread of the Gospel, through Jesus Christ our Lord, who lives and reigns and with you and the Holy Spirit, one God, for ever and ever. *Amen.*[17]

Endnotes

1. *The Book of Common Prayer* (New York: Oxford University Press, 1990), p. 229.

2. Ibid., p. 380.

3. Stanley Hauerwas and William Willimon, *Lord, Teach Us: The Lord's Prayer and the Christian Life* (Nashville, TN: Abingdon, 1996), p. 28.

4. Frederica Mathewes Green, "Re: The Scholar and the Church," e-mail to the author, May 29, 2007.

5. Daniel G. Woods, "Re: The Scholar and the Church," e-mail to the author. April 12, 2007, 3:08 PM.

6. Masayuki Sawa, "Re: anniversary," e-mail to the author, May 20, 2007.

7. John Christian Wenger, *Separated Unto God* (1951; repr. Harrisonburg, VA: Sword and Trumpet, 1979), p. 108.

8. Masayuki Sawa, May 20, 2007.

9. Masayuki Sawa, "Re: difficult reflection," E-mail to the author, May 25, 2007.

10. Hauerwas and Willimon, *Lord, Teach Us*, p. 29; *Resident Aliens: Life in the Christian Colony* (Nashville, TN: Abingdon, 1989), p. 170.

11. Hauerwas and Willimon, *Resident Aliens*, p. 171.

12. Gwynne, Geoffrey, "Re: scholar and church," e-mail to the author, May 24, 2007.

13. Gwynne, Geoffrey, Personal interview, May 29, 2007.

14. Gwynne, Geoffrey, "Re: scholar and church," e-mail to the author, May 24, 2007.

15. Hauerwas and Willimon, *Where Resident Aliens Live: Exercises for Christian Practice* (Nashville, TN: Abingdon, 1996), p. 91.

16. Woods, "Re: The Scholar and the Church," e-mail to the author, April 12, 2007, 3:44 PM.

17. *The Book of Common Prayer*, p. 241.

CHAPTER TEN

Worshipping with "Christian America"

A Historian's Search for a Spiritual Home in Mainstream Evangelicalism

John Fea

T he subject of the "Christian Academic and the Church" is a very personal one for me. When I first started to ponder what I would like to say, I originally thought I would discuss, in very general and ecumenical language, the ways that believing academics of all varieties might actively engage in lives of service to their local congregations, denominations, and the church universal. That, after all, seemed to be what the assignment called for. I quickly realized, however, that I just couldn't do it. I had difficulty thinking about intellectual life and the church apart from my own Christian experience. Though I am pretty sure that what I have to say may resonate at some level with those who have not shared my same religious journey, I concluded, in that moment when postmodern angst meets the tradition of Christian confession, that I would address this topic somewhat anecdotally and autobiographically.

The Scandal of the Evangelical Mind, Mark Noll's call for evangelicals to worship God with their intellects, appeared in 1994, my first year of graduate school.[1] At the time, this was exactly the kind of book I needed to read. I felt that Noll was writing to me. Though I was very much formed by the ethnic, working class Roman Catholic Church, I had converted to evangelicalism when I was fifteen, attended a college that was positioned somewhere along the rather blurry line separating evangelicalism and fundamentalism, and had two degrees from a mainstream evangelical divinity school. By the time I arrived in graduate school, I was having difficulty reconciling my pursuit of a PhD in American history with my evangelical faith. Noll put into words what I had been thinking about for a long time and inspired me to forge ahead, both as an evangelical and an academic. There was, indeed, hope for people like me.

Partly because of Noll's book, evangelicalism went through a bit of an intellectual revival in the 1990s. News of this revival even made it onto the cover of the *Atlantic Monthly*, the coffee-table magazine of choice for upper-middle class professional and intellectual types.[2] Money was out there to fund the scholarly work of openly Christian scholars. Evangelicals were finding seats at the so-called academic table. I was enthused about these developments, and though I was never invited to participate directly, many of these initiatives sustained me from afar during my graduate school years. For example, I remember when the first issue of *Books and Culture* arrived in my mailbox. I devoured its content. I joined a group of young evangelical scholars who were using the new medium of e-mail to converse with others interested in the budding world of Christian ideas.[3] It was a heady time for all of us. These were the kind of conversations we had all yearned for in the secular darkness of our graduate school programs.

And then we got jobs, settled into real communities, some of us had kids, and, like all good American evangelicals, went out to "shop" for a church. What I learned very quickly through this process was that Noll's "scandal of the evangelical mind" is still with us. As my family settled on a fairly typical evangelical church in our town, I realized that I had been in the ivory tower too long. After two very formative years as a Lilly Fellow in Valparaiso, I was re-entering a religious world for which I should have been more prepared. Few in my church had ever heard of Mark Noll or his book. Neither did they particularly care about cultivating an evangelical mind, especially if such a pursuit somehow distracted them from their "personal relationship" with Jesus Christ. Granted, Noll inspired a new generation of evangelical scholars and post-secularism has opened a door for evangelical voices in the academy and the public sphere. But when we think about an evangelical academic's place in the *church*, we also need to remember that we are a very miniscule portion of the millions of evangelicals in America today. I might add that over 90 percent of evangelical college graduates did not attend one of the movement's many fine Christian colleges.[4] My own church experience suggests that the trickle-down effect of Noll's book has been virtually non-existent in mainstream evangelicalism.

Who are these people that I encounter each week in church? What exactly do I mean when I talk about "evangelicals?" We can define them according to belief and practice. Historian David Bebbington has suggested that evangelicals affirm the importance of a conversion experience; the urgent need to fulfill the Great Commission (Matthew 28) by spreading the gospel to others through evangelism; the God-inspired Bible as the primary source of Christian revelation and guide to holy living; and the importance of Jesus Christ's atoning death on the cross for the sins of the world.[5] If understood in this basic fashion, I would imagine that there are many individuals who might identify with the evangelical faith, despite the fact that they find their ecclesiastical homes in other Christian traditions.

When I call myself an evangelical, I certainly affirm Bebbington's tenets, but the church I attend is also a part of what George Marsden has called the "evangelical denomination."[6] This, of course, is not a denomination in the traditional American Protestant sense of the term, but rather, it is a religious subculture, made up of a variety of local church members connected to one another in real and imagined ways. The evangelical denomination, for example, is held together by a *common language* (evangelicals talk about when they were "saved," they share their "testimonies" with one another; and they encourage fellow believers in their "walk with the Lord"). The evangelical denomination is also held together by the authority of identifiable spiritual leaders and writers, such as Rick Warren, Max Lucado, John Stott, Charles Stanley, J. I. Packer, Chuck Swindoll, and Beth Moore. It finds outlets for worship and entertainment in a catalog of music that includes traditional hymns, praise songs, and Christian pop. It includes non-denominational para-church organizations (such as Campus Crusade for Christ, Samaritan's Purse, or Wycliffe Bible Translators) and Christian radio shows (such as those hosted by James Dobson, Chuck Colson, and Joyce Meyer). It has its pope— the Reverend Billy Graham. And it has its Vatican—Wheaton, Illinois. (Colorado Springs and Orlando have recently challenged Wheaton's position of supremacy. Is an evangelical "Great Schism" in the works? I doubt it.).

This is a subculture, as historian Joel Carpenter has argued, that emerged in the decades following the 1925 Scopes Trial, when fundamentalists were ousted from the public square and forced to retreat into their own religious enclaves.[7] Only within the past thirty years or so has it been mobilized into a political force in American life. Much of this "denomination" has attached its hopes for America to the Republican Party. It is adamantly pro-life and anti-homosexual, it insists that we need to reclaim the Christian roots of America (more on that below), and it wants creationism (or intelligent design) taught in public schools, but only after the school day opens with Christian prayer. To be fair, not all members of the evangelical subculture embrace all of these positions. But in general, those who embody this "denomination" are the people that Noll had in mind when he wrote about the "scandal of the evangelical mind."

It never ceases to amaze me just how many of today's Christian academics were raised in the evangelical subculture. These scholars reconcile their evangelical pasts with their intellectual pursuits in a variety of ways. Some abandon Christianity completely because of scars they received from their fundamentalist childhoods. Most that I know, however, do not go that far. Instead, they leave the evangelical denomination. Some remain evangelical, but worship in mainline Protestant churches. Others convert to Catholicism or Orthodoxy. Most continue to uphold, to one degree or another, Bebbington's evangelical tenets, but reject—sometimes rather harshly—the subculture that has been formed around those tenets. You can find these people, I might add, in humanities departments at most evangelical colleges affiliated with the Council for Christian Colleges and Universities.

Let me say up front that I am very sympathetic to the spiritual journeys of some of these former members of the evangelical subculture. Like Noll, there is rarely a day I do not think about leaving the denomination myself, but as historian Ronald Wells has once quipped, there is no place to send a letter of resignation. As my wife could tell you, I spend a lot of time decrying the evangelical mega-church and its embrace of consumerism, its use of marketing techniques, its subtle anti-Catholicism, and its unyielding commitment to Protestant individualism. It still annoys me, crank and curmudgeon that I am becoming, that each Sunday, my fellow worshippers saunter into the sanctuary, carrying a freshly brewed cup of Starbucks coffee that they just picked up at something my church calls "Coffee Central." This past Memorial Day weekend, I perked up with a sense of promise when one of the members of the pastoral staff announced that it was Pentecost Sunday. Finally, I thought, a reference to the church calendar and an understanding of Christian time that I cherished so much about my life as a young Roman Catholic. Needless to say, I was more than a bit disappointed when the pastor used the next twenty minutes not to explain the meaning of Pentecost in the history of the church or the importance of the Holy Spirit in our lives, but instead used the pulpit for a lesson on patriotism. I am continually frustrated by the failure of my fellow believers to allow Christian conviction to shape the way they view the world and the way they conduct their everyday lives, particularly their economic lives. I am convinced that evangelicals need to learn important lessons from mainline Protestants, Catholics, and the Orthodox about the richness of the liturgy, the corporate dimension of the Church, the spiritual power of the sacraments, and the intellectual resources available in the history of Christendom.

So, by this point, some of you may be asking, why am I still an evangelical? Some of you might even feel sorry me and the things I put up with in my church life (the religious equivalent of having a 4–4 teaching load). Other may just think I am crazy not to pack my bags and move on. Yes, despite my constant criticisms, I have firmly decided, at least for the time being, not to go the route of many of my humanities colleagues who have left the subculture. My decision to stay is a complicated one that has been shaped by many factors, but if pushed, I would say that I worship with Christian America because I have a sense of calling that the evangelical subculture is where God has placed me. The people I worship with every Sunday are "my" people. I feel, as Wendell Berry might say, part of the evangelical "membership." I may, at times, be the rebellious brother or the black sheep of the family, but I am a member of the family nonetheless.

Perhaps more importantly, I can honestly say that my spiritual life is fed through the extended weekly proclamation of the Bible by a gifted expositor. I find myself profoundly attracted to the deep piety of my fellow evangelicals, who long to experience God in sometimes powerful ways. I believe that the cross of Christ has real and transforming power to radically change the lives of those who embrace it by faith. I relate to John Wesley's Aldersgate experience, when his "heart was strangely warmed." I am moved by evangelical hymns, and I even enjoy singing praise songs when they are grounded in some of the more worshipful Psalms. And I want my children to be raised in this culture. Perhaps I am biased here, but it seems that evangelicals do youth ministry better than most.

So what is an evangelical like me to do? Is there a place in this denomination for someone who, to paraphrase intellectual historian James Turner, prays like an evangelical, but thinks like a Calvinist, a Catholic, a Lutheran, or an Anglican?[8] While I find myself at home among the spiritual lives of evangelicals, as you can imagine, I also feel marginalized and distant from many who attend my local church. I share many evangelical moral positions, but I can easily be perceived as the village heretic when I express views that do no conform to all of the political, economic, theological, or historical beliefs of my friends and fellow worshippers. I would like to think, but perhaps I am wrong, that many of my so-called "heretical" views are actually informed by the kind of Christian thinking that Noll exhorts us to carry out in the *Scandal of the Evangelical Mind.*

The sense of marginalization that I feel intersects directly with my own discipline when it comes to the belief, popular among many evangelicals, that America was founded as a "Christian nation." As a historian of colonial and revolutionary America who teaches at a Christian college, I am asked constantly to address this question, both publicly and privately. I remember the first time I suggested to my Messiah College course on the American Revolution that one would be hard-pressed to argue that America was, indeed, a uniquely Christian nation. One of my students reported that her roommate, a woman who attends my local congregation, was shocked to hear that I did not believe that America had Christian roots, or that most of the founding fathers were born-again. Faculty members from the sciences and professional schools who attend my church have held me at arms length because I have gone on record saying that the Christian America argument is weak and, frankly, bad history.

These anecdotes might seem surprising. Does American evangelicalism seriously embrace this distorted view of history? The simple answer is yes. And what is more unfortunate is that some perceive those who do not uphold this view as being somewhat "less Christian" or, even worse for a member of the evangelical subculture, a "liberal."

While I do have conversations with members of my congregation about the religious beliefs of the founders, the ceremonial deism of the founding documents, the establishment clause of the Constitution, and the First Amendment, this sort of hostility became clear to me when I spoke on this topic at a local retirement home with a large population of evangelicals. I remember the events vividly. I prepared a talk that would, at least in my view, annihilate the Religious Right's faulty history. I was prepared to flood them with evidence to suggest that America was not a Christian nation, and that the founders did not ever perceive it that way. After I presented my case, I began to field questions.

I knew that most of my audience would not agree with me, but I also thought that, after forty-five minutes, they would crumble under the weight of scholarly evidence and come around to my view. The questions were polite, and most of the crowd showed a great deal of respect for me and what I shared. But it was clear that I had ruffled too many feathers and come down too hard on my audience. I am sure that my air of superiority and intellectual arrogance alienated many.

As I thought more about that talk, as well as other personal and public engagements with evangelicals who held this view of America's past, I was saddened. My sorrow, however, did not come from feeling bad for all these people who were in error and didn't realize it. Rather, I was saddened because these were my people. God had placed me in their midst. Back in New Jersey, and Philadelphia, and Deerfield, Illinois, there were people just like them who had nurtured me in my faith and prayed for me regularly. Though I thought their view of American history was wrong, and perhaps even dangerous, I realized that the way I approached my topic was also wrong, if not a bit dangerous.

I learned a valuable lesson that night about how I should go about serving my church as a Christian scholar. I still engage in conversations about what I believe to be my fellow evangelicals' faulty view of history, but I am now more mindful, by God's grace, about guarding my tongue, my attitude, and my approach. For example, I try to take time to balance my conversations and formal talks on the founding with the important role that religion played in eighteenth-century society. I elaborate on the spiritual values and even "family values" that some early Americans upheld. I talk about the piety of Jonathan Edwards or George Whitefield or John Wesley or Charles Finney and what we evangelicals might learn from their examples about how to live Christian lives. My critiques have become more subtle—they take the form of questions, rather than browbeating lectures. While such an approach might fail to pass muster in the academy, even the Christian academy, I have found that this may be the only way of connecting with my fellow evangelical believers on some of the issues that have, up until now, been an important part of my intellectual life.

In the end, many of my struggles as a Christian scholar in the evangelical denomination are probably quite similar to the kinds of difficulties all Christian academics—evangelical or not—face as members of local church communities. It seems that we need more Christian scholars, especially those in the humanities, an enclave of the academy where criticism reigns supreme, to serve the people in their congregations and become actively involved in the lives of those with whom they disagree on some of the vital issues of the day. This does not mean that we should stop using our training and gifts to educate the church or challenge them to apply Christian thinking to all areas of their lives, but it does mean that we should engage in the often difficult practice of Christian humility, piety, and hospitality as we do it.

I will end with what St. Paul says in Romans 12 (and I might add two things: First, evangelicals simply refer to the author of this passage as "Paul," and second, I will be quoting the New International Version, the translation of choice for most of my fellow evangelicals):

> Do not think of yourself more highly than you ought, but rather think of yourself with sober judgment, in accordance with the measure of faith God has given you. Just as each of us has one body with many members, and these members do not all have the same function, so in Christ we who are many form one body, and each member belongs to all the others…

Endnotes

1. Mark Noll, *The Scandal of the Evangelical Mind* (Grand Rapids, MI: Eerdmans, 1994).

2. Alan Wolfe, "The Opening of the Evangelical Mind," *The Atlantic Monthly* (October 2000).

3. Many of these scholars have recently teamed up to write *Confessing History: Christian Faith and the Historian's Vocation,* John Fea, Jay Green, Eric Miller, eds. (Notre Dame, IN: University of Notre Dame Press, forthcoming).

4. Allen Guelzo, "Cracks in the Tower," *Books and Culture* (July/August, 2005).

5. David Bebbington, *Evangelicalism in Modern Britain* (London: Routledge, 1989).

6. George Marsden, *Evangelicalism and Modern America* (Grand Rapids, MI: Eerdmans, 1984).

7. Joel Carpenter, *Revive Us Again: The Reawakening of American Evangelicalism* (New York: Oxford University Press, 1997).

8. James Turner, "The Evangelical Mind," *Commonweal* (January 15, 1999).

CHAPTER ELEVEN

Dual Citizenship

The Politics of Belonging to
Church and Academy

Scott Huelin

For some years now, theologians such as Stanley Hauerwas and John Milbank have labored to identify new metaphors for thinking about the nature of the church, ones that would move beyond the moribund Lockean notion of church as voluntary association of likeminded individuals. To my mind, the best alternative yet has been the idea of the church as *polis*, that is, a distinct community organized around a common good and defined by certain practices and virtues. If the church is a *polis*, then so is the academy. And if this is so, then those who identify themselves as Christian scholars know both the blessings and the frustrations involved in dual citizenship. Though a simple observation, it demands some unpacking.

I am no expert on immigration law, but I am told that dual citizenship, i.e., holding the full privileges and obligations of citizenship in two different countries simultaneously, is a relatively recent phenomenon. Up until the 1970s, American law considered citizenship as an exclusive privilege; one could not be unswervingly loyal to America while also maintaining a formal allegiance to some other country. In fact, up until that time, Americans who applied for citizenship in some other country were regarded as having renounced their American citizenship automatically, and immigrants seeking to be naturalized as U.S. citizens were required to forswear all foreign allegiances. Thus, the concerns raised about John F. Kennedy's Catholicism during his presidential campaign were not simply the product of knee-jerk Protestant parochialism (though such attitudes certainly played a role): From the perspective of American immigration law, Kennedy's loyalty to a foreign power (in this case, the Vatican) was a legitimate obstacle to his faithful American citizenship, let alone the successful execution of the duties of President.

Today, U.S. immigration law and policy have relaxed quite a bit: The State Department acknowledges, but does not encourage, dual citizenship, and the foreign naturalization of a U.S. citizen no longer automatically entails the handing over of one's U.S. passport. This should come as no surprise in our rapidly globalizing world, where borderless markets have usurped the place of nation-states as the ultimate shapers of identity and community for many. In such a climate, it may be difficult for us to understand why there was such institutionalized anxiety about dual citizenship. This anxiety, though characteristic of Euro-American modernity, actually has its roots deep in the ancient world. Witness Plato's argument in Book 8 of the *Republic*, where he claims that certain kinds of political constitutions produce specific kinds of character in its citizens. A Spartan, as a member of a timocracy, was almost certainly going to be a trained warrior and inveterate honor-lover, while an Athenian, as a member of a democracy, would most likely be a lover of words and pleasures, and therefore not a particularly good warrior. In much of the ancient world, the notion that "statecraft is soulcraft" was axiomatic. One internalizes the political constitution in which one is formed; i.e., *polis* begets *ethos*. To put this in more contemporary terms, power produces subjectivity (and thus it turns out that even Michel Foucault is but a footnote to Plato). If it is the case that politics effectively shapes character, then dual citizenship, to someone like Socrates, would have seemed a particularly debilitating form of schizophrenia; this may help us understand why he opted for death over exile from his beloved Athens.

This close connection between *polis* and *ethos* may also help us better understand Tertullian's famous rhetorical question: "What has Athens to do with Jerusalem?" I doubt that Tertullian thought he had merely coined a clever synecdoche for the disagreements between pagan and Christian teachings. Rather, Tertullian knew that a *polis* or a community organizes around a commonly identified good; that its social structures and practices provide both access to, and enjoyment of, that good; and that its citizens develop certain habits and dispositions that enable and motivate their participation in the life of the *polis* and its shared good. Put differently, Tertullian knew that any *polis* has its *doctrina,* as well as its *disciplina*; its set of teachings or beliefs, as well as the social instruments for producing citizens who not only share, but embody these beliefs. Thus a *polis* always embodies some notion of wisdom, when wisdom is understood as an account of the order of things and a way of life that seeks to harmonize with that order.[1] While Jerusalem and Athens do, indeed, have different wisdoms, this difference manifests itself first and foremost in their divergent ways of life, their disparate politics.

St. Augustine, too, thinks of Christian identity along political lines. In his monumental *City of God*, he defines a city as "an assembled multitude of rational creatures bound together by a common agreement as to the objects of their love."[2] On this account, the City of God is a transnational, trans-temporal community comprised of those human beings and angels who name the Triune God as their highest good and live according to a pattern of corporate life that both establishes and nurtures the double love of God and neighbor. Augustine goes on to contrast this city with another, the earthly city, in which self-love rules, begetting a lust for the domination of others. According to Augustine, neither of these cities can be identified with any particular human institution: Rome is not, itself, the earthly city, though it does participate in this ideal polity; nor is the Church the heavenly city, though it does instantiate that ideal polity on its better days. Even though these two cities have no territory to guard, they may come into conflict. Oaths of allegiance or sacrifices to Roman emperors were, from very early in the Church's history, understood as challenges to the exclusive obedience demanded by the Lord Jesus, and vice versa.[3]

Given the evident disparity in value between the two cities as Augustine presents them, we would be foolish to consider the two citizenships compatible: "Friendship with the world is enmity toward God" (James 4:4). In order to be faithful to the heavenly city, in which we cannot now fully dwell, we must merely pass through the earthly, keeping ourselves free from the authority and discipline of its politics. Hence Augustine's constant recourse to metaphors of peregrination to describe the heavenly city's relation to the embodiment of the earthly city in the Roman empire. But isn't this way of negotiating the demands of the two cities less than fair? After all, Augustine is juxtaposing the ideal type of the city of God with the concrete manifestation of the earthly city. How would the picture change if we considered the competing claims upon our loyalty that are made by two human institutions? Would the contest between church and academy be as easily decided as those between the two ideal cities or between one ideal and one concrete city? Can one hold dual citizenships in these two institutions, or does naturalization into one entail renunciation of the other? Can the two natures of *homo academicus* and *homo ecclesiasticus* inhabit the one person of the academic Christian?[4] In order to begin to answer such questions, we will have to examine the distinctive virtues produced and demanded by the constituent activities of church and academy, as well as the effects of each upon the other.[5]

What, then, are the constituent activities of church and academy? Central to the identity and mission of the church, in all its many instantiations, is the activity of *worship*. It is difficult to imagine a church that does not gather regularly to praise, pray, and preach, to baptize and break bread; a church devoid of common worship would, in effect, be no church at all.[6] But the practices of Christian worship provide us with far more than the "marks of the church," important as they are. Common worship is the instrument by which the Holy Spirit forms this new community, shaping in its members the virtues required of a particular alternative society. As John Howard Yoder used to say, the church is God's politics. Think of the variety of worship practices that identify the various denominational traditions because they nurture distinctive patterns of virtue in their practitioners. For example, those traditions which make preaching central seem especially good at fostering obedience; it is no accident that so-called "divine command" ethics arises out of the Reformed tradition. Similarly, worship centered on the Eucharist seems particularly effective in forming hospitable Christians, as the frequent partnerships of high-church traditions and social justice ministries in contemporary America suggest.[7] The fasts of the church year provide, for the traditions that keep them, an excellent school for patience, because absent alleluias make the soul just as hungry as missed meals do the body, and learning to bear hunger in hope is the better part of patience. Thus, it is no exaggeration to claim that "liturgies *are* our effective social work."[8]

Among the church's wide range of worship practices, and of the moral virtues formed thereby, we may tentatively discern a certain unity across traditional lines. All of the practices and virtues mentioned above seem to converge in forming and enacting varieties of *responsiveness* in the Christian worshiper: responsiveness to God (in praise, gratitude, and obedience), responsiveness to other people (in hospitality or forgiveness), and responsiveness to the temporal structure and contingent nature of human existence (in patience). Though we may logically distinguish these three capacities for response by means of their respective objects, we rarely experience them separately. Seeing the face of Christ in the suffering neighbor, welcoming the stranger as the Father has welcomed us, bearing hardships as loving parental discipline: Each of these recognizably Christian responsivities indicates the mutual implication of these three relational domains while testifying to the primacy of the first. Common worship, the school of praise, shapes our responsiveness not only to God, but also to others and the world we inhabit, for worship "is the point of concentration at which the whole of Christian life comes into ritual focus."[9] Doctrine and life, love and loss, work and play also have the praise of God as their end, and it is through gathering for the explicit purpose of praise that we become able to see, much less live, this truth. In the Great Thanksgiving that is worship, Christians everywhere return to God what is rightfully God's and, in return, receive these things anew, freshly restored to their creaturely purpose of praise.[10] In responding rightly to these gifts, we respond rightly to their giver; thus, gratitude and praise reinforce and deepen one another, making worshipers out of the consumers, hedonists, and nihilists we might otherwise continue to be.

The academy, of course, centers upon a different activity, and thus, it demands and fosters a different set of virtues from and in its participants. But which activity plays a constitutive role in the academy analogous to the role of worship in the church? Though the academy has altered its aims and methods innumerable times over the centuries, fundamental to all genuine instantiations of the academy has been the activity of *inquiry*. I take inquiry to mean both the disciplined formation of questions and the equally disciplined search for their answers. The formation of questions includes not only the genesis of a question in wonder or puzzlement, but also the careful refinement and reframing of questions over a lifetime, within a discipline, or throughout a tradition.[11] The search for answers to such questions involves not only the formulation of hypotheses, but also the communally-normed practice of weighing putative answers and discerning better ones from worse. Put historically, the activity of inquiry depends upon the traditional practices of rhetoric, dialectic, and disputation.

Inquiry, as I have described it, requires at least one virtue of its practitioners, namely *thoughtfulness*. As an intellectual virtue, thoughtfulness is reflective engagement, the kind of thought that makes questions possible through its capacity for wonder, and that also makes critique possible through its assessment of answers. Thus, thoughtfulness makes inquiry excellent by its manifest care for particular things and the connections among and between such particulars, by its determination to settle for only the most compelling account of them by rigorously weighing the outcomes of inquiry, and by its insistence that no genuinely human question has ever been exhaustively answered. In short, it is the virtue of thoughtfulness that makes the liberal arts *liberal*. In inquiring well, we liberate ourselves from our own and others' unexamined opinions, thereby freeing us for the pursuit of better opinions, and thus, of truth.

Yet this liberty is not without its price. While thoughtfulness is a requisite virtue for the excellent practice of inquiry, left to itself, it can also undermine that very same activity. For the liberal arts require leisure, that is, a temporary retirement from necessary work in order to make time for reflection. Liberal education thus demands, as an inflexible prerequisite, the liberation of the student from the demands of particular communities and projects which have heretofore constituted her life, that is, from her *polis*. In the American system of higher education, this prerequisite is manifested quite literally and physically in the residential requirements still in place in most liberal arts institutions. Before any abstract thought begins, the student already has been abstracted from her *polis*, her formative community, and placed in a new *polis* with comparatively few social obligations and virtually no common project; thus, abstraction begets abstraction, *polis* begets *ethos*. Perhaps this explains why Nietzsche's derisive characterization of liberally educated men in nineteenth-century Germany retains much of its force in our own day. Such men, Nietzsche observes, carry within them "enormous heap[s] of indigestible knowledge-stones"; they are "wandering encyclopedias" who have only meta-knowledge and no knowledge that is truly their own; they become "restless, dilettante spectator[s]" whom "even great wars and revolutions cannot affect ... beyond the moment."[12] Doesn't this description capture much of the cynicism, detachment, restlessness, inattentiveness, and intellectual satiety among our own students?

In the academy, the intellectual virtue of thoughtfulness is all too infrequently accompanied by the moral virtue of thoughtfulness, what we might describe as a concern for the particular joys and sufferings, needs and desires of particular individuals, as the kind of responsiveness that is best learned in a *polis*. Without the support of a complementary virtue, one that instantiates the other-directedness so often lacking in the contemporary practice of inquiry, our academic work readily degenerates into systematic disillusionment of self and others. At its worst, this tendency is manifest in the all-too-familiar phenomenon of instructors gleefully demolishing their students' unreflective parochialisms. Thoughtfulness without other-regard seems unlikely to rise above sardonic voyeurism and disinterested vivisection. Left to its own devices, *homo academicus* is not a pretty sight.

Responsiveness, though, needs inquiry just as much as inquiry needs responsiveness; otherwise, our response may well be misdirected, disproportionate, or poorly resourced. The chief danger of training people to worship is that they may easily become idolators. Our Anglo-Saxon word "worship" literally means to ascribe worth to some object, and of course, there are many objects to which we middle-class Americans ascribe worth, thanks to the politics of the market. Thus, our comparatively well-appointed worlds provide innumerable provocations to, and practice in, idolatry, that is, ascribing undue worth to a lesser good. These goods need not be merely material; think of the various fetishes with which American Christians seem particularly enamored: On the right, there is Bibliolatry, familyolatry, megachurcholatry, and Busholatry, while the left provides us with rightsolatry, empowermentolatry, and Democratolatry. If no one can serve two masters, why do so many Christians seem content to serve four or more? *Homo ecclesiasticus* is, indeed, a many-headed hydra.

Persons who are involved in meaningful ways in real communities, ones gathered around a common good, defined by common practices, and marked by common virtues, need the discipline of thoughtfulness that comes with liberal arts training, that enables one to step back from such projects and practices in order to understand them, and where necessary, to reform them. But when the academy so habituates its students into abstraction as a disposition that it liberates its students *from,* rather than *for,* meaningful involvement in real human communities, when they become intellectual peregrines or "walking encyclopedias," then we have failed to model for them and nurture in them the virtue of responsiveness that most of us learned in church. And so it seems that *homo academicus* and *homo ecclesiasticus* not only *can* dwell together in unity, but that they *must* do so in order to fully achieve the good which each one seeks. Dual citizenship, in at least this case, proves essential, rather than detrimental, to each *polis's* particular interests. If Jerusalem and Athens are, indeed, to meet on one fair campus, they will do so first of all in the person of the academic Christian who bears the marks of each *polis* in her own *ethos.*

Endnotes

1. See Pierre Hadot, *Philosophy as a Way of Life* (London: Blackwell, 1995).

2. Augustine, *City of God* 19.24.

3. See, e.g., *The Acts of Perpetua and Felicitas*, c. 200 AD.

4. The term "homo academicus" was coined by Pierre Bourdieu; see *Homo Academicus*, trans. Peter Collier (Stanford, CA: Stanford University Press, 1988).

5. An earlier version of the next few pages was first read as part of a paper entitled "Personal Integration" delivered at the *Faith in the Academy* conference, Messiah College, September 2004.

6. Especially in light of New Testament Greek, in which "church" is *ekklesia*, those who are "called out" of the world into an alternate community. See, e.g., 1 Peter 2:9–10.

7. Cf. 1 Corinthians 11:20–22.

8. Stanley Hauerwas, *The Peaceable Kingdom: A Primer in Christian Ethics* (Notre Dame, IN: University of Notre Dame Press, 1983), p. 108.

9. Geoffrey Wainwright, *Doxology: The Praise of God in Worship, Doctrine, and Life* (New York: Oxford University Press, 1980), 8 and *passim*.

10. Alexander Schmemann, *For the Life of the World: Sacraments and Orthodoxy* (Crestwood, NY: St. Vladimir's Seminary Press, 2002), *passim*.

11. Josef Pieper, *Leisure: the Basis of Culture*, trans. Alexander Dru, 2nd ed. (New York: Pantheon, 1964), pp. 69–82.

12. Friedrich Nietzsche, *The Use and Abuse of History*, trans. Adrian Collins (New York: Macmillan/Library of Liberal Arts, 1957), pp. 23–24 and 29.

Keynote Address

CHAPTER TWELVE

Embracing Wisdom

Mark R. Schwehn

For my morning devotions, I use the Benedictine prayer book called *The Work of God*. The order for Monday morning prayer includes the following reading from the book of Sirach, a piece of wisdom literature decreed by both the Orthodox church and the Roman Catholic church to be canonical and included by most Protestants as part of the Apocrypha. The reading is as follows:

> My child, from your youth chose discipline, and when
>   you have gray hair
> You will still find wisdom.
> Come to her with all your soul, and keep her ways
>   with all your might.
> Search out and seek, and she will become known to
>   you; and when you get
> Hold of her, do not let her go.
> For at last you will find the rest she gives, and she will
>   be changed into joy for you. (Sirach 6:25–28)

Many, probably most, academicians today, even if they were to agree with the representation of wisdom in this passage, would object to the idea that the quest for wisdom is the proper business of the college or university. In the declining number of universities where there remains a robust sense of common purpose, faculties would be more likely to describe their collective project as the pursuit of specialized knowledge, or the advancement of science, or service to society through scholarship, teaching, and professional formation. Wisdom would seem to most of them an ambition that is too exalted and vague at best, and far too archaic at worst, an old-fashioned piety that smacks too much of morality or religion, or both.

This supposed linkage between religion and the quest for wisdom led David Ford, the Regius Professor of Divinity at Cambridge University, to worry recently over the future of his university in a 2003 lecture that some of us who have been part of the Lilly Fellows Program have read together under the title, "Knowledge, Meaning, and the World's Great Challenges: Reinventing Cambridge University in the Twenty-first Century."[1] Ford was speaking from the vantage point provided by his three-year term of service on the University's Personal Promotions Committee, which required him to read all of the papers submitted about every candidate put forward for a personal professorship or readership by every faculty and department of Cambridge. The worries that arose from this experience and his reflections upon it were not borne of nostalgic longing for a lost age of Christian orthodoxy nor of a hankering for the return of the earlier restriction of admission to Cambridge to those of the Anglican faith. On the contrary, Ford noted with approval the fact that Cambridge had needed to reinvent itself at least five times during its eight hundred years, and that it surely would and should do so again in the near future.

Ford's worries instead stemmed from his own conclusion that Cambridge's major challenges involved the sustenance and reinvention of the collegiate system, the improvement of teaching, interdisciplinarity, transgenerational responsibility, and the inseparability of questions of knowledge from questions of meaning and value, a series of challenges best summed up, or so he thought, as a renewed quest for wisdom, a quest that had to be guided, in his judgment, by the great traditions of wisdom, both secular and religious. Just three years before Ford spoke, however, the Regents of Cambridge had adopted a statement of core values that made one striking and unfortunate omission. Though the statement mentioned the importance of "sport, music, drama, the visual arts, and other cultural activities," it failed to mention religion. And so it seemed to Ford that, just at the moment that the university most needed the wisdom of *multiple* traditions of thought and practice, it had mysteriously and arbitrarily cut itself off from several of the oldest and richest of them.

In closing his address, Ford drew from another Biblical image of wisdom that shares with the image in the book of Sirach its feminine character, though the figure in the Song of Songs is much more elaborately and sensually drawn. In the midst of this description, the poet exclaims, addressing wisdom, "Your neck is like an ivory tower" (7:4). Ford wondered what the university would be like if it were to seriously and purposefully anchor its aspirations in such imagery, if today's ivory tower really were a vital part of wisdom. We shall have occasion later to ponder the significance of the feminine figuration of wisdom in these ancient books. For now, we might think together about what warrants Christians in the ivory tower might have for construing their enterprises as quests for wisdom.

I believe that there are at least three such warrants, and they come to us all in the form of our titles or degrees, our spiritual/geographical location, and, no surprise here, our vocations. We all bear the degree PhD, with all the rights, privileges, and honors thereunto appertaining—and the duties and responsibilities, as well. Doctor of philosophy means literally that we are, or should be, lovers of wisdom, for this degree long antedated the period when philosophy became just another one among other academic disciplines. Instead, philosophy then meant the passionate pursuit of the truth of matters high and low, human and divine, natural and cultural, and it surely entailed a search into the nature of things, into the meaning of the whole. Unless and until we are prepared to regard the titles we bear and the gowns we wear as merely the quaint reminders of a time far away and long ago, we should strive to live as best we can in vital communion with the tradition that gave rise to those titles and vestments. We should strive, even in the midst of our specialties, as well as within the larger community of which those specialties are a part, for wisdom.

Our second warrant comes to us by virtue of our spiritual/ geographical location at the intersection of the ways to and from Athens and Jerusalem. If Socrates were here, of course, he would have long since invited us to wonder whether wisdom *can* be taught before we inquired into whether it *should* be. And he would, as well, have insisted that we cannot know whether wisdom can be taught unless and until we know what wisdom is. Rather than seeking to define it, we should, for now, agree with David Ford in thinking that we belong to more than one tradition of wisdom, and that most of us belong especially to two of them. And they are distinct, they sometimes conflict, and at best, they stand in creative tension with one another. In the introductory chapter of his book *The Beginning of Wisdom*, another occasional reading in the Lilly Fellows Program, Leon Kass draws the distinctions between Athens and Jerusalem very sharply.[2] According to Kass, Athens grounds wisdom in the powers of human reason, whereas Jerusalem does so in the fear of God, and in awe and reverence in God's presence. For Athens, the eye is the primary sense organ of wisdom; for Jerusalem, the ear is primary—first to hearken unto God's commands, later to hear the good news of the Gospel. For faith commeth by hearing, and hearing, by the Word of God.

We could, of course, multiply and refine these distinctions. Instead of doing so at present, however, I should like to make only two brief observations about the place of wisdom within the various discourses of the academy today. First, over the course of the last twenty years or so, wisdom has become a subject of research among several of our colleagues in the social sciences, especially among psychologists and educationalists. You might have read about, for example, the Berlin Wisdom Paradigm, developed and refined at the Max Planck Institute for Human Development. Though this research is far from conclusive, marked by fierce debates among scholars in the U.S. and Europe, some degree of broad agreement has emerged. Wisdom, most contemporary social scientists think, involves not only cognitive, but also affective and moral dimensions of human life. Though this will not come as news to those of you here who have studied wisdom through engagement with classic texts, you should, I think, resist the temptation to be condescending or dismissive toward your colleagues here and abroad who are now seeking to measure wisdom, and even to test for it. After all, this kind of research, dressed up in footnotes, mired in controversy over research methods, and featuring the development of intricate machinery for empirical testing, is the sort of thing that is more likely to put wisdom on the explicit agenda of the academy at large than invocations of Aristotle or Aquinas. I, for one, am all for enlisting allies wherever we can find them.

And second, however conflicting the Athens and Jerusalem traditions of wisdom may be, they are both equally opposed, though for different reasons, to the comparatively narrow tradition of scientific rationality that governs and informs so much of higher learning today. It is this latter and relatively new tradition of human thought that is so often indifferent, if not hostile, to the quest for wisdom, being suspicious of inquiry into the nature of things. Worse still, and this is a development that is peculiar to our own times, many professionals who are guided exclusively by this tradition of modern, scientific rationality, threaten to make human beings over into the very flat and soul-less creatures that their science imagines them to be. Here is how a seasoned observer puts the matter:

> Today, our view of genuine reality is increasingly clouded by professionals whose technical expertise often introduces a superficial and soulless model of the person that denies moral significance. Perhaps the most devastating example for human values is the process of medicalization through which ordinary unhappiness and normal bereavement have been transformed into clinical depression, existential angst turned into anxiety disorders,

and the moral consequences of political violence recast as post-traumatic stress disorder. That is, suffering is redefined as mental illness and treated by professional experts, typically with medication. I believe that this diminishes the person, thins out and homogenizes the deeply rich diversity of human experience, and puts us in danger of being made over into something new and frightening: individuals who can channel all of our desires into products available for our consumption, such as pharmaceuticals, but who no longer live with a soul: a deep mixture of often contradictory emotions and values whose untidy uniqueness defines the existential core of the individual as a human being. When this happens the furnishings of our interior are no longer the same, we are not the same people our grandparents were, and our children will not be the kind of people we are.[3]

In brief, the search for wisdom today is by no means merely academic, so to speak, if it ever was. The stakes of inquiry are very high, and the participants in that inquiry should be very broadly inclusive.

We come finally to the third possible warrant for us as Christian academics to seek wisdom in our work together, namely, our sense of vocation. Of the many readings we have considered over the years in the Lilly Fellows Program colloquium on the subject of vocation, my favorite one comes from Dietrich Bonhoeffer's *Ethics*.[4] Writing in the midst of a threat to humanity even graver and more urgent than the one we face today, Bonhoeffer insisted that we Christians have but one call, and that is the call to follow Jesus unconditionally. From our own vantage point, this call becomes our responsibility, a responsibility exercised through, and limited to some extent by, our socially defined work, but extending always to a care for the whole of humankind. Bonhoeffer dwells for some time on those comparatively rare cases where we must, in order to heed the call of Christ, go beyond or break through the narrower specifications of our professions to exercise our responsibility for the whole. He uses the example of a doctor who, he says, will carry out her vocation for the most part at the bedsides of patients in her care. But she and all Christian physicians must, Bonhoeffer insists, be ready at times to stand up for medicine itself, for the science behind it, and for public health, even if this means putting the narrower understanding of professional responsibility at risk.

Just so with us. We will and we should spend most of our time working within the narrower domains of our specialties and sub-specialties. But we must, especially in these times, be ready to stand up for the good of our disciplines, and of the larger field of higher learning of which these disciplines are parts, for, in other words, the continuing search for wisdom. In doing so, we must be ready, even eager, to join hearts, hands, and minds with others who may not share our religious convictions, but who do share our longing for wisdom and truth and our love for fundamental and enduring questions about the shape and meaning of our lives and destinies. The man whom I just quoted about the perilous condition of our times happens to be a secularized Jew, Arthur Kleinman, who currently serves as Chair of Anthropology at Harvard, and whose field is medical anthropology. His most recent book, entitled *What Really Matters*, explores, through a series of marvelous biographical sketches drawn from his clinical practice, what it means to live a moral life amidst uncertainty and danger. Too often, those of us who, like me, are prone to despair over the present condition of the academy in general, or over the condition of a particular academic discipline, ignore the self-corrective powers of the academy at its best. I believe that the great questions are irrepressible, as is the search for wisdom. When one department, or guild, or discipline abandons altogether concern for the fundamental questions in favor of merely technical and fashionable or lucrative and trivial pursuits, some other departments, or groups of scholars, or individuals like Kleinman take up these questions with renewed vigor and precision. As I have written elsewhere, the great divide within higher education today is not between the secular academy and the church-related academy. It is, instead, between those who remember and cherish those traditions of wisdom that justify the university at its best and those who have forgotten or who willfully ignore them. Again, we must join with our allies wherever we find them.

W hat other implications might there be for our thought and practice if we come to think that a proper understanding of our vocations as Christian teachers and scholars impels us to frame our work within the academy as seeking wisdom? I have already spoken about our need to become more responsible academic citizens, caring for the good of the whole. Let me mention, before I close, three more practices that I think are essential if we seek wisdom for ourselves and seek to cultivate it in others.

First and last, worship—both private, daily devotions and regular attendance at a local parish or the college's or university's chapel. Though we may stand at the intersection of Athens and Jerusalem, we must incline finally toward Jerusalem and the heavenly city. And if we think that wisdom begins in the fear, love, and trust in God, we should know that those spiritual virtues have their home and their sustenance in the church through liturgy and the practice of corporate worship.

I must thank Jeff Zalar for my own growth in the practice of daily prayer. When Jeff came to Valparaiso as a Lilly Fellow and I was asked to be his mentor, he said he wanted to focus upon spiritual exercises, not upon academic issues. I have always suspected that he figured out early on that he was not going to learn much from me that he did not already know about the craft of historical scholarship, and that he therefore hoped I might be a spiritual director. He soon discovered that, though I might be an occasionally successful pinch hitter, I was even less capable and qualified in the area of spiritual formation as I was in the area of history. But this was all to the good in a sense, since it meant that Jeff and I embarked on this journey together, discovering and assigning books to one another (I remember our first reading was Alexander Schmemann's *For the Life of the World*), finding and sharing liturgical materials for daily prayer, discussing how the practice of daily prayer enriched our academic lives, and holding one another accountable.[5] Had it not been for Jeff, I doubt that I would have been so eager to spend a year's leave at the Benedictine St. John's

University, nor would I have found there the prayer book that I mentioned at the outset of this talk, *The Work of God.*[6] And so it is that what, for me, began in prayer, the germinal idea for this talk, comes round to focus upon prayer as most important on the way to wisdom.

It may well be that the Lilly Fellows Program, partly because of my own ignorance of and relative inattentiveness to matters of worship and prayer, has for too long neglected systematic attention to the place of worship within the church-related academy. I pledge to do what I can during the next phase of our common life to focus more diligently and thoughtfully, in both word and deed, upon this question. And I think we should all wonder together about the character, the place, and the opportunities for worship on our various campuses. This, too, is our collective responsibility, even if that responsibility falls more heavily and more properly upon some than upon others.

A second practice that we must undertake, I think, is to maintain breadth of vision, even at the same time as we narrow our focus in our scholarship. You will all have your favorite ways of doing this, of keeping up with the larger conversation of the academy with itself and its publics, but I try each week to read both *Books and Culture* and the *New York Review of Books* pretty much from cover to cover. I don't always succeed, of course, but aspirations are important. I regard this exercise less and less as a matter of achieving breadth of vision, and more and more as a matter of finding friends on the way to wisdom, people like Arthur Kleinman, for example. And I need not tell this group that the quest for wisdom must be a communal undertaking before it can become an individual aspiration.

Third and finally, I think we must learn first to discern, and then to encourage and strengthen those students who already show signs of wisdom. It should come as no surprise to you, though it did come as something of a surprise to some of the aforementioned social scientists, that wisdom is not at all directly correlated with intelligence of the sort that can be measured on IQ tests and that often shows itself in the preparation of clever, sometimes even brilliant, papers within a given specialty. Many of us tend, I think, to gravitate more to the bright students than to the wise ones. And I think we must learn to correct for this tendency to some extent. I suggest we do so by broadening the range of students who habitually engage our extra attention and care, and by resisting the temptation to lavish excessive attention upon those who show the greatest promise as future practitioners of our own favored disciplines.

These recommendations of attention to academic citizenship, worship, intellectual friendship, and formation are sometimes bundled together at both secular and church-related colleges and universities today under the rubric "educating the whole person." Though this formulation arose initially under Jesuit provenance, it has since been adopted by student service people and others all over the country, most of whom have no idea of the rich tradition of thought and practice that gave rise to it. The *point* of "educating the whole person" has been lost, and its anchorage in the Christian tradition has been largely forgotten, leaving only a somewhat anemic, trendy, and vaguely therapeutic vocabulary where there was once spiritually robust understanding. Intercollegiate athletics, yoga, and wellness courses are, as a result, claimed by many to be equally important to a college education as the study of mathematics, history, or a foreign language. Are we not better advised to speak in the vocabulary of wisdom, thereby reminding ourselves always of the purpose of our common endeavors? And does not that vocabulary best capture what we and those communities of learning that we serve might be at our best?

In bringing this inquiry now to a temporary close, let me admit that I chose my title, "Embracing Wisdom" to imply a partial critique of the book of Sirach's meditation upon wisdom, one that has implications, I think, for how we might finally understand our own vocation as lovers of, and seekers after, wisdom. Whereas there are, as I remarked earlier, many virtues and advantages in representing wisdom by the figure of a woman, there are some disadvantages, as well. These disadvantages are more obvious, perhaps, in the book of Sirach than they are in the Song of Songs. Notice that, in the passage I quoted at the outset of my remarks, readers are exhorted to "search out and seek" wisdom, "and when you get hold of her do not let her go." This is the language of masculine conquest softened only by the final line, "For at last you will find the rest she gives, and she will be changed into joy for you."

This vocabulary of seizure and possession should apply to wisdom if, and only if, the movement between wisdom and those who seek her is reciprocal. I therefore chose to entitle my remarks with the *double entendre* "Embracing Wisdom," which, on the one hand, describes wisdom as the one who does the embracing, and on the other hand, describes the aim and activity of those who seek her. We must and we do believe that the One who is Wisdom seeks out and embraces us before we seek to embrace Wisdom. As Kierkegaard put it in *Training in Christianity,* "For it is not as though we must hold fast to Christ; rather, it is Christ who holds us fast, now and even forevermore." This embrace is the very embrace that is both the beginning and the end of all of our seeking and finding, and it is the embrace that gives us the freedom to pursue our inquiries, our own various quests for truth, with a wild abandon—knowing that we are held fast, even as we strive to possess the Truth that possesses us.

What happens, we might wonder, if and when we come into full possession of that wisdom that we love and seek? Does our love of wisdom cease once our desire for it has been *fully* satisfied, once we live wholly and completely in the presence of God? Such a thing cannot happen in this world, of course. Even so, the book of Sirach teaches truly here when it says of wisdom, "For at last you will find the rest she gives and she will be changed into joy for you" (Sirach 6:28). This is just right. You find what you have first been given. And when you find it at last, your longing for knowledge and truth will then be met by a Good appropriate to it. Such a culmination can only give way to delight in the perfect marriage between desire and its object, even as restlessness gives way to rest. And so it is, and so it must be, that at the last embrace, wisdom will indeed "be changed into joy for you."

When you are fully and completely at work in your callings as seekers of wisdom, you will sense intimations of this everlasting joy, foretastes of the feast to come, as it were. In the midst of those small transactions of everyday academic life, you really will, from time to time, figure something out, discover some part of the truth about the world, catch a fragment of the logos, see the flicker of light in the darkness. And when this happens, you will have an evanescent sense of the deep joy that can be fully known only in eternity. May we all sense something of that joy in one another's company, now and often thereafter during the course of our life together as pilgrims on way to wisdom.

Endnotes

1. David Ford, "Knowledge, Meaning, and the World's Great Challenges: Reinventing Cambridge University in the Twenty-first Century," *Studies in Christian Ethics* Vol.17, no. 1 (2004) 22–37.

2. Leon R. Kass, *The Beginning of Wisdom* (New York: Free Press / Simon & Schuster, 2003).

3. Arthur Kleinman, *What Really Matters: Living a Moral Life Amidst Uncertainty and Danger* (New York: Oxford University Press, 2006), pp. 9–10.

4. Dietrich Bonhoeffer, "The Place of Responsibility" in *Leading Lives That Matter: What We Should Do and Who We Should Be*, Mark R. Schwehn and Dorothy C. Bass, eds., pp. 107–111 (Grand Rapids, MI: Eerdmans, 2006). Also see *Ethics* in *Dietrich Bonhoeffer Works, Vol. 6* (Minneapolis, MN: Augsburg Fortress Publishers, 2004), pp. 289–297.

5. Alexander Schmemann, *For the Life of the World* (Yonkers, NY: St. Vladimir's Seminary Press, 1997).

6. Judith Sutera, *The Work of God: Benedictine Prayer* (Collegeville, MN: Liturgical Press, 1997).

On the Contributors

Joseph Creech received his PhD in history from the University of Notre Dame. He teaches history and humanities in Christ College at Valparaiso University and specializes in American cultural, political, and religious history. In 2005, he was named one of the notable "Young Scholars in American Religion" by the Center for the Study of American Religion and Culture. He is the author of *Righteous Indignation: Religion and the Populist Revolution* (Illinois, 2006).

Kathleen Sprows Cummings (Lilly Postdoctoral Fellow, 1999–2001) is Assistant Professor of American Studies at the University of Notre Dame. She is also the Associate Director of the Cushwa Center for the Study of American Catholicism and holds concurrent appointments in the departments of history and theology. Her teaching and research interests include the history of women and American religion and the study of US Catholicism. Her first book, *New Women of the Old Faith: Gender and American Catholicism in the Progressive Era*, appeared this year (2010) with the University of North Carolina Press. Cummings recently received a National Endowment for the Humanities Fellowship to support her current work on a new book project, *Citizen Saints: Catholics and Canonization in American Culture.*

Martha Greene Eads (Lilly Postdoctoral Fellow, 2001–2003) studied literature and theology at Wake Forest University, the University of North Carolina at Chapel Hill, and the University of Durham (UK). Her research and teaching interests include twentieth- and twenty-first-century drama, English modernism, and contemporary Southern fiction, and her articles on those topics have appeared in *Christianity and Literature*, *The Cresset*, *Modern Drama*, *The Southern Quarterly*, and *Theology*.

John Fea (Lilly Postdoctoral Fellow, 2000–2002) is the Chair of the History Department at Messiah College in Grantham, PA. He is the author of *The Way of Improvement Leads Home: Philip Vickers Fithian and the Rural Enlightenment in Early America* (University of Pennsylvania Press, 2008) and *Was America Founded as a Christian Nation: A Historical Introduction* (Westminster/John Knox Press, 2011), and the co-editor of *Confessing History: Explorations in Christian Faith and the Historical Vocation* (University of Notre Dame Press, 2010).

Paul Harvey (Lilly Postdoctoral Fellow, 1993–1995) is a Professor of History and Presidential Teaching Scholar at the University of Colorado at Colorado Springs. He is the author of *Freedom's Coming: Religious Culture and the Shaping of the South from the Civil War through the Civil Rights Era* (University of North Carolina Press, 2005), as well as the blogmeister for "Religion in American History" at http://usreligion.blogspot.com.

Thomas Albert (Tal) Howard (Lilly Postdoctoral Fellow, 1997–1999) teaches history at Gordon College, where he also directs the Jerusalem & Athens Forum, an honors program in the history of Christian thought and literature. He is the author of several books, including *Protestant Theology and the Making of the Modern German University* (Oxford, 2006) and *God and the Atlantic: America, Europe, and the Religious Divide* (Oxford, forthcoming in 2011), and he is the editor of Mark Noll and James Turner, *The Future of Christian Learning: An Evangelical and Catholic Dialogue* (Brazos, 2008).

Scott Huelin (Lilly Postdoctoral Fellow, 2001–2003) received his BA and MA from the University of North Carolina and PhD from the University of Chicago. He was a member of the Christ College faculty at Valparaiso University from 2002 to 2009. He currently serves as Associate Professor of English and Director of the Honors Community at Union University in Jackson, Tennessee.

Maria LaMonaca (Lilly Postdoctoral Fellow, 1999–2001) is an Associate Professor of English at Columbia College. In 2008, she published her first book, *Masked Atheism: Catholicism and the Secular Victorian Home* (Ohio State University Press, 2008). Currently, she is co-editing (with Leslie Haynsworth) a collection of essays on ambivalent personal responses to Victorian novels, entitled *Vexed by the Victorians: Twenty-First Century Reverberations of Nineteenth-Century Fiction*. She lives in Columbia, South Carolina, with her husband John Wisdom, her son Robbie, and her daughter Cecilia.

James Paul Old is Editor of *The Cresset*. He received a BA in Political Economy from Hillsdale College and an MA and PhD in Political Science from the University of Notre Dame. He teaches courses in political theory and American politics at Valparaiso University.

John Steven Paul was Program Director of the Lilly Fellows Program in Humanities and the Arts and Professor of Theater at Valparaiso University, until his passing in 2009. He also served as Director of Valparaiso University's touring liturgical drama group Soul Purpose.

Mark R. Schwehn is the Provost of Valparaiso University. He has taught at the California State University at San Jose (1969–1972), the University of Chicago (1975–1983), and in Christ College, the Honors College of Valparaiso University (1983–2009), where he was dean from 1990–2003. His publications include *Exiles from Eden: Religion and the Academic Vocation in America* (Oxford, 1993), *Everyone a Teacher* (Notre Dame, 2000), and with Dorothy C. Bass, *Leading Lives That Matter* (Eerdmans, 2006).

Colleen Seguin (Lilly Postdoctoral Fellow, 1996–1998) received a BA in History and English from Mount Holyoke College and an MA and PhD in History from Duke University. At Valparaiso, she serves as Chair of the Department of History and teaches European history and humanities classes. Her article, "Ambiguous Liaisons: Catholic Women's Relationships with their Confessors in Early Modern England" in *Archive for Reformation History*, won the Jane Dempsey Douglass Prize of the American Society of Church History in 2006.

J. Michael Utzinger (Lilly Postdoctoral Fellow, 1999–2000) is Associate Professor of Religion at Hampden-Sydney College in Virginia. He is the author of *Yet Saints Their Watch Are Keeping: Fundamentalists, Modernists, and the Development of Evangelical Ecclesiology, 1887–1937* (Mercer University Press, 2006). He is currently writing on the role of religion in the Prince Edward County, Virginia school closings between 1959–1964 and working on a biography of the Rev. Charles R. Erdman, a key figure in the fundamentalist controversies within the Presbyterian church. Utzinger serves as Associate Director of the Hampden-Sydney College Honors Program and was recently Chair of the Religion Department.

Heath White (Lilly Postdoctoral Fellow, 2003–2005) received his PhD in philosophy from Georgetown University in 2002. He is currently Assistant Professor of Philosophy at the University of North Carolina-Wilmington. He has published articles on philosophy of mind and practical reason in several professional journals, and he is the author of *Postmodernism 101: A First Course for the Curious Christian* (Brazos Press, 2006).

Jeffrey T. Zalar (Lilly Postdoctoral Fellow, 2002–2004) is a historian of Modern Germany and Central Europe. His publications address nationalism, confessional conflict, and Catholic intellectual culture. He teaches at the University of Wisconsin-Whitewater.

In memory of

John Steven Paul
1952 – 2009

Program Director
Lilly Fellows Program in
Humanities and the Arts
2005 – 2009

Index

academic guilds, 42, 49; as sources of freedom and protection, 39; rights, privileges, and responsibilities, 51–52

academics; as citizens, 108; as members of congregations, 91–92; friendship and, 12–13; in the public square, 15, 21–22; private study and, 11; within the Catholic Church, 79

academy, the. *See also* higher education; inquiry central to, 110

Acts, Book of, 84

Alliance for International Monasticism, 17

American Historical Association, 35

American Magazine, 76

Anglicanism, 118

Appleby, R. Scott, 66

Aristotle, 121; *Ethics*, 15

Arnold, Matthew, 5

Association of American Colleges and Universities, 23

Association of Catholic Colleges and Universities, 79

Athens and Jerusalem (as metaphor), 9, 31, 32, 33, 107, 112, 120, 121

Atlantic Monthly, 73, 96

Barber, Benjamin R.; *Jihad vs. McWorld*, 61

Barnabas, 84, 87, 92

Bass, Dorothy; *Receiving the Day*, 49

Bebbington, David, 97

Bebel, August, 72

Benda, Julien, 15

Benedict XVI, 61

Berger, Peter; plausibility structures,

Day, Dorothy, 66
Dochuk, Darren, 34, 35
dual citizenship, 105–106
Duke University, 90

Eastern Mennonite University, 87,
88, 89
economic reductionism, 7
ecumenicism; in scholarship, 8
Edmunds, Henry, 71
Eliot, George, 47; *Middlemarch*, 46
Ellison, Ralph; *Invisible Man*, 36
Episcopal Church; role of scholars
in, 91
Erasmus, 14
Eucharist, 109
Evangelical Lutheran Church in
America, 24
evangelicals, 9; as a denomination,
97–98; as scholars, 96, 98–99;
churches, 96–97; defined, 97;
in politics, 98; intellectual
resurgence among, 6, 96; neo-
evangelicals, 7; understanding
of American history, 101–102;
what they can learn from other
traditions, 99; vitality of, 100

fasting, 109
Fea, John, 34
feminism; defined, 78; new
feminism, 77
Ferguson, Niall, 5
Ferrum College, 85, 86
First Things, 74
Fish, Stanley, 6
Focus on the Family, 36

Ford, David, 118, 120; "Knowledge,
Meaning, and the World's
Greatest Challenges," 118
Foucault, Michel, 57
Fox, Margaret Fell, 25
France; German occupation of,
52–53
Franchot, Jenny, 43
Freedman, Estelle; *No Turning Back*,
77–78
friendship, 14–15, 18; relationship to
study, 12–14
fundamentalism; Christian, 7;
Islamic, 60
fundamentalist; modernist debate,
8, 98

Gage, Matilde Joslyn, 72–73
Gandhi, Mohandas Karamchand, 64
Geertz, Clifford, 62–63, 67
Gilman, Lawrence, 73
Glory (film), 36
God; work of, 84
Goff, Philip, 33
Gospel Advocate, 73
Great Commission, 97
Griffith, Marie, 35
Gross, Terry, 61
Guerin, Mother Theodore, 78–79
Gwynne, Geoff, 91–94

Hailandière, Celestine de la, 78–79
Harris, Sam, 61
Hart, D. G., 7
Harvey, Paul; *Freedom's Coming*,
33; *Themes in Religion and
American Culture*, 33